The Encyclopedia Of Parenting From A-Z

So Help Me God!

Dr. Carol S. Kennedy

KENNEDY
PUBLISHING
SERVICES

P.O. BOX 51518
FORT MYERS, FL 33994-1518
WWW.DRCAROLKENNEDY.COM

ISBN# 0-9702741-0-6
(Third Printing 2004)

Dr. Kennedy conducts seminars on topics related to
parenting, education and literacy.
drckennedy@aol.com

Table of Contents

Dedication

To my Dad,
who's always meant the world to me.
I love you Dad!
Thank you for your guidance, teaching and discipline

Lovingly,
Your daughter,

Carol

Acknowledgements

Special thanks to my husband, Dick, for his unending encouragement of me and my pen along this writing journey.

More thanks to daughter Stacey as she innocently provided the material for a large percentage of this book's content.

Thanks to the hundreds of school-age children and their parents over the past three decades who supplied me with the proof of the importance of effective parenting.

Foreword

Kids haven't changed, parenting has…and not always for the better.

There are too many kids walking around without discipline or an acceptable code of behavior. It is the job of the parents to instill discipline and appropriate behavior.

If you ever wonder how important parenting is, just look around your neighborhoods and schools. We can view the products of effective and ineffective parenting wherever we go: Just watch the children.

Over the past three decades, I have learned that parents not only need help; they want help. Children seek guidance and direction, and if they do not get it from the parents, they will find it elsewhere.

This book offers pointers for parents on subjects ranging from "How to Teach Respect," to "Nobody Wins the Blame Game."

Good luck!

Introduction

Parenting is one of the most important jobs we will ever have and yet it still comes without instructions. *The Encyclopedia of Parenting From A-Z, So Help Me God!* offers some answers. *From A-Z* is a collection of short parenting articles, each approaching a unique topic of parenting. The topics are issue-and value-driven, ranging from "R-E-S-P-E-C-T" to "Clean Your Room."

From A-Z gives parenting back to the rightful owners: the parents. Once parents reclaim responsibility for parenting, they should move it to the top of their priority list. Faith and social organizations offer assistance; however, parenting is best done by parents. The author's belief system may be summed up this way: Discipline is a gift, give it to your child, wrapped in love and care.

Recurring themes are: The parent is the child's first teacher, as the home is the child's first school; children so desperately need and want the discipline that effective parenting delivers. If guidance and direction are lacking in the home, children will seek discipline in places where it may be counterproductive.

From A-Z offers a special blend of experience, expertise and common sense. This mixture yields informative, easy-to-read, practical tips for raising children.

A unique feature of this book is a special section entitled, "Crack the Code." To Crack the Code is to unlock the phonetic code of our language. To unlock the phonetic code is to decode. Once children can decode they begin to experience the joy of translating the printed symbol into meaning. They can read! Each article concludes with a "Pointers for Parents" section, which outlines steps to incorporate the parenting technique into the home. During especially hectic times the readers can proceed directly to the "Pointers for Parents" section for quick information.

Since parenting leaves lasting imprints on our children's hearts, we need to take the time to do it right. Let's enjoy our children for the short time they are under our care.

THINK ABOUT THIS

Becoming a parent is easy. Being one is difficult.
Discipline is a gift. Give it to your child.
To discipline is to love, care, help and direct
children along the path of life.
Without it, there is no direction.
Children will invent their own.

When we discipline our children, we give them
the confidence and courage they need to make the right
decisions.

Yours in the interest of effective parenting,

Dr. Carol Kennedy

Part One

Parenting From A-Z

So Help Me God!

◆◆◆◆◆◆◆◆◆◆◆

♦ AMBIVALENCE IS OUT ♦

Confusion reigns when parents treat children with ambivalence. Ambivalence is when children ask one question and get two answers: one from each parent. With ambivalence comes uncertainty, contradictions and unclear expectations. The roadmap for behavior is blurred.

When parents are ambivalent, children choose either to ignore both answers, or to pick the one they like the best. Kids learn at a very early age to use the "pick and choose" tactic to their advantage. Once kids know ambivalence has set in, they begin the pick and choose method.

<u>EXAMPLE:</u>
CHILD: 'Mom, Dad, can I spend the night with Bill on Friday?'
MOM & DAD (yelling from different rooms): Mom—'I said you couldn't spend the night until you pick up your room.'
DAD: (simultaneously): 'Oh sure, what time do you want to go…?'
Whoops! That's ambivalence: One question, two answers.

Both parents realize simultaneously what happened. The child has just received two answers to the same question. Now what does the child do?

We can sense the confusion the child feels when the parents disagree on an issue.

WHAT SHOULD HAPPEN: At the point of ambivalence the parents say: 'Time out, we have to discuss this . . .'

When Mom and Dad are on the same page with parenting issues, the children have stability, certainty, continuity and clear expectations. Kids know when they will get one answer to one question.

When parents are unsure of an answer sometimes they reply: 'I don't know; go ask your dad/mom!' If this happens in your family, just remember: If you tell the child to seek an answer from the other parent, accept the answer as the final one. If you don't, ambivalence takes over again.

POINTERS FOR PARENTS
HOW TO AVOID AMBIVALENCE

1. Mom and Dad should DISCUSS THE BASICS of parenting before communicating them to the children.

EXAMPLE: Take the issue of drinking soda. Should we allow the kids to drink soda or not, and if so, how often?

Mom and Dad should discuss how they feel about the soda issue, the consequences of overindulgence, and the frequency of consumption: a soda once a week; once a month?

As soon as Mom and Dad agree, tell the children. They cannot read our minds.

2. CONSULT YOUR SPOUSE. If a situation arises and you are unsure how your spouse feels, tell the kids: 'I'm not sure, I'll check with your mom/dad.' This usually gets a loud groan from the kids. Now, they know they can't play the ambivalence game with you, and will get one answer to each question.

3. PREDICT the changing needs/questions of the kids. Your teen will want answers to teen questions concerning dating and

driving the car. Be sure you and your spouse discuss these issues before the questions are asked.

4. DISCUSS PARENTING ISSUES you feel strongly about. Maybe you feel strongly about certain dating aspects. Relay concerns to your spouse before they arise in the family.

REMEMBER: Kids need stability, certainty, continuity and clear expectations. With ambivalence, kids get contradictions and uncertainty. To avoid ambivalence, discuss aspects of parenting with your spouse. When kids ask one question, they need one answer.

♦ OUR OWN BACK YARD ♦

Remember the saying: 'Sometimes what you're looking for can be found right in your own back yard.' I've been reminded of that lately as I discover friendship, honesty and old-fashioned values right in my own back yard.

Like many, I yearn for the good ole days when you could trust your neighbors and depend on each other to get over the occasional rough spots in life: from the very simple to the complex; from the cup of sugar to the assistance needed in troubling times.

I thought we had lost that spirit as a nation until this past summer when I discovered the heroic qualities in people living in our neighborhoods. We seemed to go from crisis to crisis this year. We were confronted with forest fires and hurricanes. In each instance there were innumerable examples of people helping people, going above and beyond the call of duty.

My faith in humanity was restored. The heroes I read about were my next-door neighbors.

We are lucky to have neighbors in Southwest Florida and Central Florida. Both neighborhoods are overflowing with caring, kind-hearted people of all ages.

In our Southwest Florida home, Hurricane Georges was a real threat. The hours of preparation brought out the best in our neighbors. They helped each other board up windows and buy food and water. The last pieces of plywood were shared. Younger neighbors helped the elderly shop, board their homes and realize they had a safe place to go if they needed one.

In our second home in Central Florida, neighbors help each other out on a daily basis. Neighbors help each other with repairs, baby-sitting and house-sitting. It is incredible and an awesome sight to behold. Neighbors are a priority and it shows every day.

My husband and I have taken it upon ourselves to be the extroverts in displaying the neighborly way in our Southwest Florida home. The residents are friendly enough when seen, but many are just plain busy in their daily lives. My husband and I feel the outward neighborly attitude is best. We make it a point to be friendly to everyone and find out about each resident.

Even though we are both busy, we have decided 'being neighborly' is a priority. As a result, we have discovered a variety of new friends and life experiences. There is a greater respect and awareness of one another. When problems arise, we all solve them together.

We've all been told and taught 'not to talk to strangers.' But once you meet and get to know your neighbors, you're no longer strangers. As a parent, we need to be cautious, but not to the point of being paranoid.

So parents, use your good judgment and common sense while being neighborly.

POINTERS FOR PARENTS

1. CHECK OUT YOUR NEIGHBORHOOD. Learn your neighbors' names and occupations. Introduce yourself and be a friend.
2. VOLUNTEER to help each other whenever it is needed.
3. Let the neighbors know you are WILLING to be a friend and to help when needed.

REMEMBER: The good ole days may be right in your own back yard. Those traits of friendship, honesty and helping each other may be closer than you think. Check it out!

♦ A NEW BEGINNING ♦

HAPPY NEW YEAR! January 1st is just around the corner. Often, the notion of New Year's resolutions is foremost in our minds. Some personal reflection takes place and we wonder how we can make the coming year a better one.

For the moment, let's assume that no one is perfect. Further, let's assume no one is perfect in the parenting department. Parenting improvement will not necessarily take more time. Improved parenting may just require a change of emphasis, direction or focus. If the children have been home for nearly two weeks there have been ample opportunities to witness what happens between the children and parents.

Choose a few quiet moments for reflection. Perhaps there were certain behaviors from the children that irritated you. Or, perhaps you noticed instances when the parents made a mistake and problems arose. Assess the situation as objectively as you can. Even if you already receive an 'A' in parenting, you may be able to earn an 'A+.'

POINTERS FOR PARENTS

1. JUST SAY NO—TO THE TV: Set limits for television viewing. Consider the 30-60 minute a day rule. Chances are, if the children are engrossed in television for endless hours, little else is taking place.
2. SCHEDULE regular reading times: Choose 15-30 minutes per day to read with or to the children. Read aloud from the child's book, or read your own book silently as the children read their book or magazine.
3. CATCH them doing good: Make a point to compliment children daily. Praise them for helping around the house or for doing their schoolwork.
4. TALK with the children: Take time daily to ask about their day. Continue to ask specific questions until you get answers. Do not settle for: "Ah, same ole stuff, you know..." Keep asking until you get a specific answer. If you are home when the children return from school, enjoy a snack together and discuss the day. When my daughter was growing up this was our favorite time of the day. A simple snack of milk and graham crackers was the catalyst for a conversation about our day. She told me about her day and I would follow, telling her about my day. It is a meaningful tradition to begin.

From the list of POINTERS select one that will work for your family. Circle it and place it on the refrigerator. When glancing at it you'll be reminded of its importance. Once you have success with the first choice, draw a star beside it. Proceed to another. As you feel the parenting behavior is improving, share this knowledge with the family.

REMEMBER: No one is perfect! As parents, we may simply need to refocus our time and energy. We can make improvements one step at a time. Good luck and good beginning!

♦ CLEAN YOUR ROOM! ♦

"**Clean your Room!**" parents shout. Children respond: "I already did!" Unable to believe what they just heard, parents mumble under their breath or reply: "How can that possibly be? There are still piles of clothes/toys all over the floor."

Does that scenario ring a bell? I can't tell you how many times I echoed those words on Saturday mornings to my child. I tried changing my tone. I tried changing the wording, thinking it would bring about a cleaner room. And of course, it didn't.

It took me a while to figure out why. I experienced frustration and confusion. I simply couldn't understand why my child didn't want a clean room. I thought I was doing the right thing as I chanted every Saturday morning: "Okay, clean your room before you go outside." She'd enter the bedroom and exit an hour later with no visible difference in the condition of the bedroom.

Finally, I had to admit something: My daughter was not entirely like me. She really didn't care if the clothes were picked up off the floor. She claimed she knew where everything was, so what was the big deal? As you might imagine, this brought a few sassy remarks from me…and more meaningless dialogue.

Frustrations mounted and it became clear: I needed a plan. How was I going to solve this, so I wouldn't go crazy before her eighteenth birthday?

I had to draw a few conclusions of my own before I devised a plan.

1. A clean room was *my* priority, not hers.

2. *My definition* of clean was obviously not the same as my child's definition.

3. I had to *teach her* how to clean her room; maybe she really didn't know.

4. Her clean room will not coincide with *my* notion of a clean room.

If you don't consider these conclusions, you will go crazy!

Once I drew my conclusions, I could devise a plan of action and, I hoped, implement the plan. **I must caution**—the same advice does not work for all families. However, there is some comfort in knowing: ***WE ARE NOT ALONE.***

I will share some techniques that worked for me.

POINTERS FOR PARENTS
THE PLAN:

1. DEFINE CLEAN: When you say 'clean your room,' what do you mean?

2. Once you've decided what you mean, TELL THE CHILDREN. It *is* true—they *cannot* read our minds.

3. DECIDE what you will *accept* as 'clean.'

4. REALIZE the 'room thing' is used as one of those ways to rebel in the teen years. If you know it ahead of time, it can ease your frustrations.

5. PLAN A DAY to show the children 'how' to clean that room. Show them what to do first, and where to put all those things that are on the floor. If we don't show them, all their stuff ends up under the bed or in the corner of the closet.

6. SHOW THEM 'how to' fold the clothes you want put in the drawers. Many kids don't have a clue how to fold clothes.

7. ANSWER ALL THEIR QUESTIONS: There's no such thing as a dumb question. The only dumb questions are those that are never asked.

OUR PET PEEVES DO MATTER!

ONE of my pet peeves was to see clothes on the floor. I had the most success when I told my daughter that I was not buying her any more new clothes until I saw a clean floor. I told her it really hurt my feelings to spend all that money on new clothes and then to find the clothes piled on the floor. She said she 'never thought of it that way before.' The condition of the floor improved tremendously.

REMEMBER: To have a clean room is usually on the parents' priority list, not the child's. I don't think I've ever spoken with a parent who was entirely satisfied with the condition of their child's room. Decide what you will reasonably accept as a 'clean room.' And admit it: your children's clean room may never *entirely* meet your expectations.

♦ COMMUNICATION'S THE KEY— AT ANY AGE ♦

Communication can be the key to a mutually enjoyable relationship. The major focus of this book is parenting; however, the skill of effective communication is needed in any relationship. The skills presented can be transferred to almost any situation you may encounter. Often when a disagreement ensues we hear the familiar refrain: "Oh, I didn't know that, why didn't you say so…" Many times we may be thinking about something but may not totally share it with the person in our relationship. Confusion and disagreement may follow. In divorce situations I have heard many partners say: "Gee, I didn't even know there was a problem." If there had been ongoing communication, there would have at least been knowledge of an existing problem or area of concern.

Communication within the family is often muddied with hectic schedules and working parents who are struggling just to accomplish the tasks of the day. Parents, you are not alone! You may be wondering: "How can I do any extra communicating when I barely have enough time as it is . . ." If you apply the following pointers, you may actually save time. In the long run, you will have more productive time to spend with your children.

POINTERS FOR PARENTS

1. TALK WITH THE CHILDREN: Take time daily to ask about their day. Continue to ask specific questions until you get an answer. Do not settle for: "Oh nothing, you know." Your first thought may be: "No, I don't know, tell me."
2. PROVIDE A RELAXED ATMOSPHERE in which to discuss the day. If you are home when the children return from school, prepare a snack. Talk around the snack, at the kitchen table or sofa. When my daughter was growing up we would have a snack together at the kitchen table and talk about our day. A simple snack of milk and graham crackers was our catalyst for a conversation. If she didn't want to talk at first, I would volunteer and tell her some highlights of my day. It must have been meaningful; when we talk long distance today, we often begin our conversation with "Well, how was your day?"
3. LOOK AT THE CHILDREN when you ask questions and when you expect a reply. Have you ever asked a question and then left the room while you wait for a reply? This can send a message of: "You don't really care about my answer, you have left the room." It is best to look at them and wait for

the answer. This sends the message that you do care and want a detailed reply.

REMEMBER: No matter what age, communication can be the cure for minor misunderstandings and it can prevent them. Take the time to talk with your children. Your day will be more enjoyable and they will feel that you really care.

♦ 'C' for CONSCIENCE ♦

Do you feel guilty when you do something wrong? Do you feel the need to make amends when that little voice keeps talking to you? If you do, that's good, you have a conscience!

Whenever I read about heinous crimes I ask: "How in the world can someone do that?" Then I remember those individuals usually do not know the difference between right and wrong or they do not care. They were never taught the difference between good and evil. They must not have that little voice inside them to lead them into good behavior. If they did, that little voice would be *screaming* to them on the way to such heinous acts.

We, the parents, are the people responsible for instilling a conscience within our children. We have our support systems such as our relatives, schools and churches to give assistance along the way. There are many books written on conscience development. Researchers do not agree on the exact moment of conscience formation. However, they do generally agree that the conscience is formed during the preschool years.

The basic definition of a conscience can be found in *Webster's Ninth New Collegiate Dictionary.* Webster defines conscience as: "The sense or consciousness of the moral goodness or blameworthiness of one's own conduct, intentions or character together with a feeling of obligation to do right or be good . . ." The key phrases in the definition are *conscious moral goodness, blameworthiness* and *obligation to do right.*

First, *moral goodness* refers to the notion that morality is ever-present in distinguishing between right and wrong. A moral person is an ethical one. Moral goodness suggests standards for acceptable, correct behavior are in place.

The second part of the definition: *blameworthiness* of one's conduct. Blameworthiness translates as 'deserving blame' for one's actions. To be able to deserve the blame one needs to possess a sense of right and wrong and accept the responsibility for an action. We only need to see the news or read the papers to listen to people blaming everyone else for their mistakes. As a school teacher and administrator since 1970 I can attest to the fact that few children accept blame for their mistakes. I call it the *Blame Game.* My husband, in his twenty-fifth year as a dean for area middle school children, witnesses the blame game daily from children and their parents. They blame the other kids, the teachers, the guidance counselors, the administrators, their parents or aunts and uncles. *The blame game* is played all around us for children to see as they are forming their conscience. That is another reason we, as parents, need to act on this issue. We have an abundance of negative competition in this area.

The final key phrase is: *obligation* to do right. For someone to have an obligation to do right they need to know what is right. Children learn what is right when they are taught what is right. Again, parents are the key teachers in this process. To have a feeling of obligation, we need to care. We need to care enough to make the right choice. While we are teaching children right from wrong we congratulate them when they do the right thing and we correct them when they do not.

POINTERS FOR PARENTS

1. Begin to teach children RIGHT FROM WRONG during the preschool years. Be direct and tell them exactly what is right and what is wrong.
2. CONGRATULATE THEM when they do something right. Correct them when they do something wrong.
3. LISTEN TO AND WATCH your children. If you hear them playing the *blame game* intercede and talk about responsibility for one's actions.
4. Don't be afraid to ASK FOR HELP from the local school, church, synagogue, relatives or friends. We all need support while parenting.

REMEMBER: A child's conscience is formed during the preschool years. As parents, we are the most important force in the child's preschool years. The rewards are astronomical when we take the time to do it right. Parenting is a tough job, but we can do it!

♦ CREATIVE PARENTING ♦

Whether you are a parent, grandparent, aunt or uncle, the basics of parenting remain the same: to lovingly give direction, guidance, encouragement and values to our children. CREATIVITY enters the picture as the parents strive to incorporate the parenting basics into different situations. Whether the situation is formal, informal, fun or serious, children still want the same thing: guidance and direction.

There are occasions for quiet time and noisy time. The quiet times are needed so children can learn to sit still, think and spend time reflecting or reading. If we should ever forget the abundance of time we were expected to be quiet, reflect back to the thirteen years spent in school! While parenting, remember to instill the necessity for quiet times as well as active, noisy ones.

It is often during the noisy, active times that parents forget the rule book. Even during these fun, active times there need to be rules and boundaries of behavior set by the parents. If the parents do not take charge, the children will, and then we have an out of control situation.

Keep in mind *if parents give no direction, children get no direction.* We do our children a favor by setting boundaries and expectations. If we do, they will eventually 'get it' and apply it later in life.

Once we establish rules and guidelines even within the activities, we are actually laying the foundation for time management and self-control. We want the refrain 'Go Play' to be joyful, not a plea for help!

THE FIRST STEP TO PLANNING SOME FAMILY ACTIVITIES:

Choose an appropriate lunch or suppertime when all the family members are home. Discuss your idea of planning activities for the entire family. As the parent, you are in charge, but insist everyone participate in the discussion. Determine first if this will be a single weekend or longer span of time.

FIRST RULE*:* One parent is the secretary. She/he writes down everything that is suggested. Later, discard the sillies and impossibles.

SECOND RULE*:* Parents do have veto power. Just explain it is one of those RHIPs: Rank has its privileges. Once children become parents, they can do the same.

POINTERS FOR PARENTS

1. DISCUSS the types of activities most family members will enjoy. Include all family members. We want them to buy into the plan. Activities could include: water activities, crafts, board games, cards, woodworking, gardening or daily outdoor picnics.

2. DECIDE what, when, where, and how. There are many details to consider and plan together: What's first? What day? What time of day? How much will it cost?

3. ALLOT a certain amount of money from the family budget. This is a great opportunity to teach the real importance of budgeting and staying within your means. That is certainly an important lesson of life.

A FEW SUGGESTIONS

1. **Play Tourist**: Wherever we live, we tend to take our surroundings for granted. Attempt to examine your hometown through the eyes of a tourist. What would they visit? What would they think is unique? Use your imagination! This activity could expand into several weeks.

2. **Renew Math Skills**: Measure a street or other area. Figure the feet and yards. While traveling, figure miles and miles per gallon. Few children know this skill. Maybe yours will be the first in their class.

WANT TO BE A SUPER PARENT? Teach your children how to make change. This is such an essential skill and few people know it. I haven't met a cashier lately who even has a clue on this one . . . Why should your children learn this? So they will not be short changed by someone who doesn't have a clue.

REMEMBER: Active play times can be great fun or great headaches. Parents have the choice and control to initiate the activities in an orderly fashion. Everyone will enjoy the time together. Plan it, play it, and enjoy it!

♦ TRUTH OR CONSEQUENCES! ♦

Remember the television show "Truth or Consequences?" As I recall watching it with my older sister, it was entertaining and we enjoyed answering the questions right along with the contestants. We laughed loudly as we ate our after school snack.

Today, as I think about the name of that show I wonder about the significance of the title. I'm quite sure younger people are unfamiliar with the show itself. I wonder how many are familiar with the 'c' word: consequences. I wonder if 'consequences' are an integral part of children's vocabulary.

While growing up, I remember the 'c' word being an important factor in *choosing* behavior. I remember thinking on many occasions: If I do this, then this will happen. If I do that, then that will happen. I *knew,* and it was made very clear in our family what the results of our actions would be. We knew the good and the bad consequences to our behavior.

For example: When I brought home my report card, I knew an A would earn me $1.00, a B, $.50, a C $.25, and forget about anything lower. It just didn't happen. However, on one occasion, I recall one of my siblings getting a D in math. All family members witnessed the lecture, the reasons given, and the disappointment in my parents' voice. The point of the story—we knew what was acceptable and what was *not.* The guesswork was gone and the conditions were clearly communicated.

Let's discuss the three key words noted in the first four paragraphs: "knew," " home" and "choose."

1. KNEW: I *knew* what the consequences would be for my behavior, before the behavior was completed. There were no gray areas. If I did what my parents had taught me to do, I would be rewarded. If I chose to do otherwise, I would be reprimanded. I knew the consequences going into childhood, and I knew them coming out.

In order to strive to do good, children need to know there are different consequences for different behaviors. Otherwise, why should they choose to excel or do good?

2. HOME: While growing up, I was fortunate to live in the same house for most of my childhood. I had a loving, safe home. It was the norm to expect to have a safe home; now it may be the exception. For example: During our three decades in the public school system my husband and I have heard children's conversations: "Where are you staying this week?" At first, we thought the kids meant "where are you staying over the weekend?" After questioning, it was clear, they meant *full-time.* They did not have one place to call 'home.' This discovery is a chilling reminder of the state of our society.

3. CHOOSE: Life is a series of choices for all of us. In order for our children to have the tools to make sensible choices, parents need to teach them the difference between right and wrong. Whether we intend to or not, actions result in consequences. The action we choose will determine the consequences.

POINTERS FOR PARENTS

1. As the parent, DECIDE THE CONSEQUENCES of your children's actions. Be firm about the rewards and punishments and communicate them to the children. Be sure to discuss the consequences with your spouse. The children need to know what to expect. They cannot read our minds.

2. Do all you can to PROVIDE SECURITY and love in your home. If you need to move, prepare the children and ease them into new surroundings and relationships. Children really need a place to call home.

3. CHOICES: Instruct the children about choices and consequences. We all make choices daily that affect people and events. Talk about good choices and bad choices. The choices we make have inevitable consequences.

REMEMBER: Consequences are a natural result of our actions. We may not always like the consequences, but they are waiting for us anyway. Help your children know the difference between good and bad choices. If they make good choices, they will experience life's rewards. This will provide a measure of psychological comfort and may minimize negative consequences for them. ENJOY YOUR CHILDREN!

♦ TWO SURE THINGS: DEATH AND TAXES ♦

That old saying is true; there are two things in life that are certain: death and taxes.

We are reminded daily of the presence of taxes, each time we make a purchase. However, we often make a conscious effort to ignore and minimize death. When we stop to think about it, we know death is imminent for us all, yet we prefer silence on the issue. It seems to be the natural, American way.

Having just lost another friend to cancer, I am reminded of the sting death brings to a family and loved ones. Whether sudden or expected, it doesn't seem to matter. Wiping the tears from my cheeks at the memorial service, I could still see the children's pain and sorrow as the minister tried to console the family and friends. Tears trickled faster each time I would glance over at the children.

They seemed to be screaming through their silence: 'She's really gone . . .will I ever see my mom again . . .what is this thing they call death . . .what will I do now . . . what will happen to me? I can't stop feeling sad . . .'

I wanted to rush over and offer comfort and assurance, but I knew I couldn't. I wanted to turn back the hands of time, but I knew I couldn't. I wanted them to have their mother back, sitting next to them, but I knew I couldn't.

And as I sat, I listened and wept. I kept asking myself: 'Is there anything that could be done to alleviate some of the pain etched into the children's faces?' I soon concluded that in any loving family the immediate shock and pain would always be there. But, maybe there is something we can do to at least prepare our family members for the inevitable.

As parents, we need to teach the pleasant with the unpleasant. We don't want to dwell on death, but somehow we need to express to our children that all humans must die and it is as natural as being born. Years ago, the elderly lived with the children and grandchildren, and often the grandparent died at home in the midst of the children and grandchildren.

As the grandparent became ill, the children saw the various stages of the illness and were taught when to expect death. Death became a natural occurrence for those families.

What can we do to teach our children that death is as natural as life, and a natural part of it?

POINTERS FOR PARENTS

1. If you attend a church or synagogue, LISTEN to their teachings and RELAY them to the children. Spiritual leaders can teach and offer comfort.

2. When a death occurs, take the opportunity to teach the children the inevitable nature of it. Instruct them that, being human, it is something we must all experience.

3. With the death of loved ones there are several stages of grief a person endures. These stages are spelled out in various books in your library, bookstore, or on the internet.

REMEMBER: With knowledge comes understanding. Just to know the stages of the grief process helps to know what to expect when a death occurs. Death is not a pleasant topic, but it is something we will all experience. The best we can do as parents is prepare and educate our children. It will help ease the pain.

♦ ENJOY YOUR KIDS ♦

Parenting is one of the toughest jobs we will ever accept. I suppose we all knew that when we assumed the responsibility. Even though it is one of the most demanding professions, it offers many rewards. It is true that with parenting come many trials and tribulations. In order to complement the demands, we must always be sure there is plenty of room for joy and fun. Our children are priceless and are only young once. Let's enjoy their presence while we can.

As parents, we are evaluated by the very words and actions of our kids. It's important as we travel down the road of parenting to arrange opportunities for joy and old-fashioned fun with our kids.

The joyful times we create will be the glue that strengthens the parent/child bond. The best advice is to be sure there is a balance in the parenting department. Be sure the guidance and growth are accompanied by enjoyment, so the child will enjoy being around you.

Once in a while take the time to just sit back and observe your kids. Do you feel your good parenting is paying off? How do your kids get along with other children and adults?

Once you've taken the time to see the effects of your parenting, build in some fun times to enjoy the kids. *Are you already thinking of some fun activities to include in your household?*

POINTERS FOR PARENTS

1. PLAY TOGETHER: Include yourself in some of the fun with the kids. Don't always send the kids to their room to play—Join in the fun, wherever it may be.

2. SHOP TOGETHER: Yes, even if the kids are in those teen years. These escapades create the most vivid memories. My teenage daughter and I struggled with this one. For a few years, I had to thoughtfully plan ahead in order to add the joy to 'mall' shopping. She always wanted the name brands, and more clothes than we could afford. My words echoed: "I don't care what the other kids are buying, you are not!" I eventually learned that I had to give a *monetary limit, and smile, smile, smile* every time we went to the mall. Then we discussed the 'need vs. want' dilemma that we all must encounter sometime in life. The pre-shopping conversations would go something like this:

Mom: "We have $70 to spend. What do you need?"
Daughter: "I need everything . . .okay . . .jeans and shirts."

Mom: "Think what we can buy for $70, not $170 . . .what do you need the most?"
Daughter: "Jeans."
Mom: "Okay, let's see if we can find some good sales and maybe we can find jeans *and* a shirt."
Daughter: "Oh sure . . . not if I get those name brands I have to have . . ."
Mom: "Let's look at other brands just for kicks . . .it will be fun . . .I think we can do it."

Of course, moms, you know I had to say this with tongue in cheek ... but I think it worked wonders.

This scenario would occur every time we would approach the subject of the mall. I never knew it affected her so **positively** until she was an adult—20 years old. She was home visiting from college and needed some jeans. While driving, she asked, "Where are some good sales, Mom? I need some jeans. And I'm not paying high prices, either!" "I don't know," I replied. She mentioned, "Let's go to Goodwill, no college kids buy new jeans anyway, only the freshmen do. If we can't find any there, let's go to the 50% off rack at the mall . . .Then maybe I can get two pairs..."

I nearly flipped! Instead of screaming joyfully, I quietly smiled, savoring the moment. I turned toward my car window and mouthed a scream of "YES!" That was proof enough for me of *the power of parenting.* I really couldn't believe it! Kids do listen, even though they may give us parents a hard time. My daughter really did pay attention, all those times we discussed 'sales.' THE POWER OF PARENTING . . .

3. READ TOGETHER: Read aloud and silently, together. Parents need to participate and are the role models. Take turns

reading aloud, a paragraph at a time. The kids will be listening to the way you put expression into your reading. Kids usually know if they need improvement in this area.

4. PLAY BOARD GAMES TOGETHER: There are plenty out there, for all ages. Shop together for a game all will enjoy. Board games provide a unique setting for thinking and conversations of all kinds. Board games can be the center of many unexpected memories. Plus, you learn a lot about each other, too!

REMEMBER: The key to happy parenting is BALANCE. Continue to discipline, teach and direct in an atmosphere of joy. Plan and participate in the fun!

♦ Football Frenzy! ♦

Fall is in the air and so is football! As a *near*-football widow, I begin to feel a twinge of irritation every fall, until I remember a few things. In our 29 years of marriage, football frenzy was *always* an integral part of our relationship. Football was a mainstay on fall weekends. Once I return football to its proper perspective, I begin to draw positive parenting tips from it.

As parents, we can view the football field as a stage for displaying parenting tips. *First,* as the mom, I had to make a decision in our family. My husband and daughter were loyal sports enthusiasts, while I preferred shopping and crafting on the weekends. I either had to be totally left out of conversations for hours on the weekend, or I could learn about the game of football. I decided upon the latter and began to choose my own favorite teams and players. I screamed for my own players and, at one point, I remember my husband commenting: "How did you know that? Since when do you like football?"

POINTERS FOR PARENTS
The benefits of any sport

TEAMWORK:
What a great advantage for the team whose players work together. Without all the players, a single player is meaningless. Teamwork can lead to greater achievement in all areas of life.

MENTAL AND PHYSICAL CONDITIONING: Sports often require the player to sustain, and to give that extra energy when they think they don't have any left. My husband instilled this in our daughter. Example: In her sophomore year, they were playing tennis. My husband grew weary and wanted to quit. My daughter retorted: "Hey, what if this was the last set and we were at a tournament; would you quit?" His own parenting words haunted him. He recalled coaching our daughter to summon that last bit of strength, and now he had to do the same. When children use a parenting technique on the parents, that's a sure sign of its power!

RISK-TAKING: In sports and many parts of our life, risk-taking is needed. Some careers demand it and some do not. PARENTS: Your wisdom is needed to discern where and when risk-taking is appropriate.

MATH: Example: football yardage, player statistics, and baseball batting averages. As a school teacher I would use the batting averages to show the relationship to school test scores. For example: When a baseball player has a batting average of .300, sports enthusiasts laud it. If a student earns a .300 on a test he has failed! A batting average of .300 is only 30 percent. Children gain a new perspective and method of learning decimals, percentages and fractions.

READING: Enthusiasm in any sport can lead to *reading* of the Sports Page. The vocabulary of the Sports Page can be challenging. Examine current biographies of your favorite athlete.

CAREERS: There are various sports careers for men and women. Our daughter was a university football team trainer. She could be heard echoing her father's advice: 'Don't quit—find that last ounce of energy!' She chose sports medicine and exercise physiology as a career.

FREE SOCIAL ACTIVITIES: An evening at home watching a football game, accompanied by snacks and good company, is an enjoyable and satisfying evening for our family.

HEROES: Americans need heroes! We are grateful to the parents of Sammy Sosa and Mark McGwire for instilling heroic values and attitudes! An amazing fact: Sammy Sosa's childhood bat was a stick; his mitt was a crushed milk carton. His ball was a mass of string and yarn. McGwire and Sosa are both devoted fathers. McGwire's son served as batboy, allowing him to be close at hand, in the dugout, witnessing his dad's moments of glory. Sosa speaks highly of his children and wife. He also extends his heroic qualities to his homeland, the Dominican Republic.

REMEMBER: Choose your sport and see how many parenting tips you can draw from it. Football frenzy can be an opportunity for family fun and discussions!

♦ FRIEND OR PARENT? ♦

During my three decades as a parent, schoolteacher and administrator, I often hear the refrain: "I'm never sure whether I should be more of a friend or parent with my children." The answer is simple: PARENT.

Once we become a parent, that is our first responsibility to our children. Raising, teaching and guiding our children are the roles of parents. Parenting should not be abdicated to the government or a village. Parenting is the direct result of something we, ourselves, have done and we must carry the responsibility through to adulthood. Does that sound too long and too difficult? Yes, it is a long time: a generation.

I don't know any other job that lasts that long, especially in this decade of outsourcing, and downsizing. If we are parents, we applied for this position; those of us who were 'hired' should take it seriously and make it our number-one priority.

Effective parenting is so important that it sets the stage for children's behavior in most situations. Parenting provides the tools for success in children's lives. Parenting is cyclical. The style of parenting we choose will most likely be the style of parenting our children will use. In essence, our parenting affects many generations. As we only have one chance to parent, we need to take advantage of it while we can.

I recall a recent conversation with a mom in her thirties whose son is two years old. She and her husband both work outside the home. She was so frazzled, stressed and seemingly overworked that she often said: "I'm so busy with work, church and housecleaning I hardly have time or patience for my son! He seems to be acting out and whining all the time!" The solution seemed simple to me as I replied: "Why do you think your son is whining and crying . . .where is your son on your list of 'to-do's'? Instead of getting what's left over of his mom he should be getting the main course." She lowered her head and replied:

"Why didn't I think of that . . .? You're right . . . I'm moving my son to number-one priority!"

Where does the 'friend' part enter into the parenting picture? The rule of thumb is: We are parents first, in a loving, *friendly* environment. When you ask "Should I discipline, guide or just be a friend?" The answer is clear—be that parent that the child so desperately needs. Right now you may be thinking about your style of parenting and whether you should make any modifications.

POINTERS FOR PARENTS

1. PRIORITIZE: Sit down with your spouse to discuss the commitment to parenting and the children as a top priority. Think and talk about issues of concern.
2. PARENT FIRST: Guide, teach and discipline in a friendly environment. You'll have plenty of time to be a friend when the children are adults living the values you instilled while parenting.
3. ENJOY THE CHILDREN: While parenting, have fun and enjoy the children. Let them know you love them and care about them. Tell them how important they are to you.

REMEMBER: Parenting is a tough job. It is one of the most important, productive experiences we will ever list on our resume of 'life.'

♦ PARENTING CAN BE FUN! ♦

Let's put the fun back into parenting. Begin planning summer fun together as a family. Start thinking about a variety of activities the entire family will enjoy. In your thoughts include some noisy, active games, as well as quiet, passive activities.

Too often, the hot summer days signal anxiety and chaos for the parents. Parents may fear the long time the children will be away from the structure of school. Parents may even begin to panic: "Oh no, the kids will be home for a very long time . . .what will I do?"

So parents, let's check our mindset. What are some of the positive, fun things we can do during the warm summer months? Parenting is one of the toughest jobs, and it can be one of the most rewarding.

Think of the summer as a great opportunity to spend more time with the children. Children need us so much; we should look forward to the extra time the summer provides the family.

A frequent comment I hear from parents is: "I really don't like the summers . . .The kids are home too long, and I don't know what to do with them." Many times, this is uttered in front of the children. How do you think the kids feel when they hear their parents echoing these sentiments? Right—not very good . . .

Be a smart parent! Begin to take control and plan ahead. The mere planning will alleviate the stress that accompanies the unknown. The one thing many children cannot handle is too much unstructured time. They may not have the skills or the maturity to know what to do with huge blocks of time throughout the day.

Remember the saying: "If you fail to plan, you plan to fail." That also applies to parenting. During many moments of my three decades of teaching, children have asked: "Why can't we have free time . . .? Every other teacher does it." Of course, my reply was usually something like "Well, if everyone else is doing it, you certainly don't need it here . . *.or* "Nothing in life is free, especially time . . ." Of course, I'm quite sure I'm the only person who appreciated that comment.

POINTERS FOR PARENTS

1. SET ASIDE A TIME all family members can brainstorm. Select one person as the recorder. In brainstorming, all answers are acceptable. Weed out the sillies later.
2. Zero in on AGE APPROPRIATE ACTIVITIES. You know what is suitable for the children.
3. Mention that you will need a VARIETY of activities: active and passive, noisy and quiet, indoor and outdoor.
4. READING should be included. This could be one of those parental suggestions.
5. LIBRARY CARD: Everyone gets a new library card. And everyone should use it throughout the summer.
6. How about WATER GAMES? This requires only a hose and some of the inexpensive attachments. This can be great fun!
7. BOARD GAMES: How about Scattegories, Monopoly, Cards, Sorry, Chinese Checkers, Scrabble? Word games are great vocabulary builders.

REMEMBER: You can put the fun back into parenting. Talk about it, plan it and enjoy participating in the various activities the family has chosen. You'll be glad you did!

♦ FAMILY REUNIONS ♦

My husband and I just returned from a family reunion in northern Michigan. I didn't know it at the time, but the reunion provided the backdrop for an impromptu display of varied parenting techniques.

Children ranged in age from 3 weeks to 17 years old. People traveled from as far north as the Upper Peninsula, and as far south as Florida: a total of 52 people. Quite a varied, random sample I would say. Four generations were in attendance.

I am happy to write that there were many good parenting techniques displayed. I was thrilled to see so many young parents showing love, guidance and direction to their children. At this reunion, the products of good parenting far outweighed the products of bad parenting.

One sure test to see if our values and good parenting 'stick' is to see how our children act when they *think* we are not looking. Do they treat other children with kindness or meanness? Do they interact in a positive manner? Do they talk and then listen? Do they fight? Are they hitting the other children?

These are simply questions to answer as you observe your children's behavior. Of course, we can expect some disagreement among children, but overall, how does your child interact with others?

Generally speaking, the evidence of good parenting I witnessed was a concerted effort of the children to get along with each other. I heard 'please' and 'thank you' often, and 'yes ma'am' and 'yes sir' spoken to adults. Or, the 'aunt' or 'uncle' was always in front of the person's name: another example of showing respect.

I heard 'I'm sorry' and 'excuse me' at appropriate times. Parents intervened to discipline and correct the children.

This impromptu display of parenting proved the importance of teaching our kids right from wrong. And so, when parents say to me: “It doesn’t matter what I do, my kids won’t listen to me,” I know that’s just an excuse. My first reply to them is: *“Tell me, what is it that you do . . .?”*

Following is a list of ***proof of good parenting.*** *Children who were products of good parenting:*

1. WERE RESPECTFUL to the adults, especially the elderly—I was impressed by the show of concern to the elderly.
2. SAT QUIETLY during the luncheon and meeting, waiting patiently for it to end. This is a normal ‘kid thing’: that children would not be thrilled about a meeting, but at least they showed respect and attempted to be quiet.
3. WERE SMILING AND HAPPY to visit other family members.
4. WERE EAGER to help younger children.

I also witnessed a few children who were *products of ineffective parenting.* These children were:

1. RUNNING AROUND all the time, not sitting for the meeting, and punching other kids.
2. NOT CORRECTED BY THEIR PARENTS.
3. MOUTHING BACK to the parents if they were told to be quiet and to sit down.

REMEMBER: Whether we like it or not, the products of our parenting, our children, are on display daily. Don’t give up—keep trying—continue to guide, discipline and teach your children right from wrong. You’ll be glad you did, and it will pay off.

♦ GIFT GIVING ♦

HOLIDAYS are a time of joy and giving, yet they can cause stress, anxiety and uncertainty in children and adults. The issue of gift giving is meant to cause joy, yet it often causes frustration. There is a way to ensure more joyful gift giving.

I have recently heard moms and dads saying, "I don't know where I'm going to find the time or the money to buy all those holiday gifts people are expecting . . ."

This parent just mentioned two of the most stressful elements of holidays—time and money. We never seem to have enough of either one! During the holiday season people often feel they cannot meet the high expectations of gift giving.

Anxieties and frustrations build. What if expectations were clarified and some boundaries were set? It seems anxieties would be lessened.

Boundaries should be set for gift giving so that everyone understands. This, in itself, will alleviate some of the stress and uncertainty. It's a good idea to set a dollar limit for gifts for family and friends. Then, everyone will be able to participate and gifts offered will be of equal value.

FOR EXAMPLE: Parents call a family meeting and discuss the idea of gift giving. A decision is made to create an agreeable price range. Then members decide if they are to buy for everyone or draw names. Parental wisdom is needed here.

When limits are set, expectations are clear. We begin to relax and enjoy the season of gift giving. Once the price limits are set, the buyers will spend less time shopping and wondering what to buy. That covers the second issue of time—some will be saved. And, of course, the plan ahead philosophy is a good one.

POINTERS FOR PARENTS

1. PLAN ahead as much as you can for your gift giving. This will diminish financial stress.
2. COMMUNICATE to the family the reason for the gift giving, whether it is a personal or religious occasion. Discuss the meaning of the gift.
3. SET GIVING LIMITS: This alleviates stress and replaces it with joy and excitement.
4. ANNOUNCE the price ranges well in advance so participants can plan according to their own personal finances.

REMEMBER: Choose joy and excitement over anxiety and frustration. Plan and then communicate the family's gift-giving decisions. Involve the whole family in the process.

♦ GRANDPARENTING ♦

ATTENTION GRANDPARENTS! Just when you thought your parenting days were over, they may have just begun! You are needed today more than ever! Your experience and expertise are in demand. You have what it takes! After all, **GRAND parenting** is merely parenting on a grand scale.

WHY is grand parenting in such demand? Grandparents are in great demand because so many children today seem to have little knowledge of family values and discipline. If kids don't know how to act, chances are they were never taught. It seems too many children lack self-control and respectful behavior. Many do not realize everything in life has limits and boundaries, including behavior. Somewhere along the line of growing up, they missed the instruction.

The easy part is determining if a child has received the proper discipline while growing up. We merely look and listen. The difficult part is infusing the skills into the child's behavior, when the parent has not. The crucial element is that the need is recognized and met.

GRANDPARENTS, you can help whether it is your grandchild or a child who needs your experience and expertise. There are two areas for you to examine—your own grandchildren or other children who may need you.

You may be thinking: 'I can't interfere with my son/daughter's ways of discipline; then they won't want me to be around my grandchildren. How do I handle that?' It's possible that your children raised their children just fine. Even if they have, you can be sure they would appreciate the support of the grandparents.

HINT: There are two ways to grandparent: your own grandchildren or other children who need you.

POINTERS

If you have grandchildren . . .

1. Shower the grandchildren with more LOVE AND GUIDANCE.
2. Offer to baby-sit for the grandchildren once in a while so you will HAVE A PART IN THEIR LIFE.
3. EMPHASIZE THE VALUES such as respect and honesty.
4. Tell them stories of 'the good old days.' ENLIGHTEN THEM with a bit of 'living history.' They usually find these stories intriguing.
5. READ ALOUD from their favorite book and encourage them to read for enjoyment.

POINTERS

If you do not have grandchildren of your own . . .

1. Look AROUND YOUR NEIGHBORHOOD. Are there any children who could benefit from your expertise? Are there any parents who seem frazzled, and could use your assistance?
2. Check the LOCAL SCHOOLS to see if they need any volunteers. Most schools will be grateful you called.
3. Call the schools or area social agencies to inquire of the FOSTER GRANDPARENT PROGRAM. The program may already be active in the elementary schools. The foster grandparents offer guidance and tutor children in need. This is rewarding for the children and the foster grandparent.

REMEMBER: GRANDPARENTING is merely parenting on a grand scale! Your skills and expertise are in great demand. Many children will benefit from your assistance, whether it is in your own family, neighborhood or area schools. Many children need that extra love and guidance that grandparents can provide.

♦ CATCH THEM DOING GOOD! ♦

As parents, we are continually teaching and directing our children. That is our job. It is one of the most important jobs we will ever have! We say: "Yes, you can and No, you cannot" innumerable times throughout the day. One of our guideposts in parenting should be to 'catch them doing good.'

It is important to accentuate the positive in all we see and do. It seems the world is overwhelmed with violence and people out of control. As parents, we need to get back our control in all aspects of raising our children. We need to directly tell them when they do right and when they do wrong. We need to keep in mind the importance of specifically and directly communicating to the children. We cannot assume that they will know what is right and what is wrong. Parents are the people to accomplish this all-important task. When we succeed as parents we will see the end product: children who know right from wrong and act accordingly. Your children will be grateful to you. My husband and I recently received a card from our adult daughter, thanking us for raising her the way we did. It brought tears to our eyes, as she acknowledged the importance of our parenting.

The basic rule is this: 'Celebrate what you want to see more of…' We can apply this maxim in the home, school, workplace or community. Think about it: The behavior we reward is the behavior we will continually see. Once we begin to acknowledge proper behavior, we will begin to see more of it. We will then witness the contagious nature of the rewarded behavior. Others will see how important this is to you, and will follow the lead. Can you see the ramifications of 'catching them doing good'? The goodness and the happiness of achievement will spread all around.

Consider your own situation: What behavior would you like to see improved? This topic can easily be transferred to the workplace or community in which you live. Once you have the skill, you can use it in many places. Think about an appropriate reward. Verbal praise is an excellent beginning. Establish material rewards as you progress. Be careful not to go overboard with the rewards. Often, parents spend so much time buying and discussing rewards, they forget the point: improving behavior.

POINTERS FOR PARENTS

1. "Clean your room!": This one is important for parental sanity. For starters, visit the child's room and discuss this issue. Demonstrate 'how to' pick up items and 'where to' place them.

BE SPECIFIC ABOUT YOUR EXPECTATIONS. Children do not know what we are thinking. Then issue a time frame: "This is what I want you to do . . .This is how to do it. I will return in 15 minutes to see how you are doing . . . If you don't know where to put something, ask me for help." A mistake some parents make is when they say 'Go pick up your room!' Then an hour later they visit the room, only to see their child sprawled out on the bed donning the headset. Once you've given the child directions on 'room cleaning' check on them in ten or fifteen minute intervals. Continue to direct them in the process as you tell them what is right and what is wrong. As children progress through the piles say: "You're doing it right! It looks so nice! It's easy to walk through the room!"

2. The dishwasher: NEED SOME HELP loading and unloading the dishwasher? Tired of being the only one in the household whose arm bends in the direction of the dishwasher? Step 1: Explain to the children the proper method of loading the dishwasher. Step 2: Clarify when to load: During the week? On weekends? After what meals? Spell it out—exactly where certain items should be placed. When they accomplish this task, CATCH THEM DOING IT RIGHT: "Thanks for rinsing the dishes and putting them in the dishwasher . . .this really helps me, and the kitchen area looks much neater."

REMEMBER: Continue to teach and direct. Continue to say 'Yes, you can' and 'No, you cannot.' When children listen and succeed be sure you *CATCH THEM DOING GOOD!* This will set a positive tone in the entire environment. You'll be glad you did!

♦ WE NEED HEROES! ♦

Heroes are a vibrant part of American tradition. They reinforce us with HOPE! Heroes come in all ages, shapes and sizes. Heroes aren't just for children; adults need heroes, too! Heroes are the visible proof that hard work and intense focus pay off. Our heroes can be people we know personally, or people we view from a distance.

We all have a sense of what a hero is, but what is it *really*? Webster's Dictionary uses the following phrases to describe a hero: "A person admired for their achievements," "noble qualities and courage"; "an object of extreme admiration and devotion."

We admire heroes for their visible accomplishments as well as their internal character and values. Heroes do not seek excellence because they want the attention. They rise above the rest because they are driven and have the desire to excel.

WHAT IS IT THAT MAKES A HERO SO SPECIAL?

Let's use the word *hero* one letter at a time:

H: **Honest** and **hard** working and **happy** to be that way! Heroes give us **HOPE!**

E: They put forth the **extra effort** to achieve their goals, and don't stop until they reach their goal!

R: Rise above the normal expectations and behaviors. They give 100% effort.

O: Outstanding in their skill or ability. They are not just average they are above all the others!

When we see a hero in action, we begin to develop an appreciation and desire for greatness. It is when a country is in short supply of heroes that a sadness pervades the atmosphere. The presence of that hero gives us a good reason to cheer and to develop a sense of camaraderie.

As parents, it is important to teach our children the meaning of heroes and to show them examples of heroes. We can certainly use history as a source of heroes or we can use the present day.

When we talk with our children about the definition of heroes, it is important to make use of 'non-examples.' In the teaching profession, use of a 'non-example' is an effective teaching tool, as it gives a clearer picture of what is a *good example*. It is simply the use of contrast in giving a definition.

FOR EXAMPLE: *"Now that we have discussed a hero, this is an example of a real hero:______________________________. And this is a 'non-example' of a hero; this is just the opposite of a hero: ______________________________________. Can you see the difference?"*

CATEGORIES & EXAMPLES:

SPORTS:

In the sports arena everyone is excited about the two baseball heroes Sammy Sosa and Mark McGwire. They have become heroes not just for their batting prowess and record-breaking ability, but also for their outstanding character and goodness. America yearns for heroes with a conscience and values.

CAREERS (LOCAL/NATIONAL):

In Central and Eastern Florida we saw many heroes in the summer of 1998 among firefighters. Their courage and strength were inspiring as the firemen risked their own lives to save others. Tears flowed from the heroes and from hundreds of people who watched their heroic actions.

CAREERS (NATIONAL):

On a national level, there are the two security guards at the Capitol building, John M. Gibson and Jacob J. Chestnut, who sacrificed themselves on July 24, 1998, so others could live. America is forever grateful to them for proving what a true American hero looks like.

Any veteran who has put his/her life on the line in defense of us and our country is a hero. There are thousands of these courageous individuals. Hats off to all of them!

QUESTION:

And what about those political figures we see and read about who are despicable and are just the opposite of a hero? We use their example to teach a lesson. We tell our children this is our *'non-example'* of a hero. This is the *opposite* of a hero. They will then understand more clearly what constitutes a true hero.

POINTERS FOR PARENTS

1. DEFINE HERO: Discuss the true meaning of a hero at the dinner table and give examples either from history or the present. Include the attributes the hero must possess.
2. CHOOSE ONE: Each family member chooses a hero and describes him/her. A photo of the hero would help so all can see what the hero looks like. The hero can be a family member or relative if they meet the definition.
3. ROLE MODEL: Stress the importance of admiration and desire to meet some of the qualifications of the hero. We may possess some of the qualities. After all, the heroes we select are merely *exceptional* human beings.

REMEMBER: We need heroes to give us that ultimate encouragement and hope. We can strive to bring a bit of that hero to our home. Heroes give us that extra burst of energy as we go about our day, cheering *with* them and *for* them! Who is your favorite hero?

♦ HOLIDAY HELP ♦

Whether you are parents, grandparents, aunts or uncles, this article's for you!

Christmas, my favorite time of year, is just around the corner! It is the same date every year, and yet we still feel overwhelmed. Besides the shopping, wrapping, decorating and baking, the children will be home for the Christmas vacation. You may be wondering: How will I be able to entertain the children?

First of all: RELAX AND BEGIN TO ENJOY the extra time you will have with your children. Vacations can be a special time for you and your children. It is a great opportunity to become closer to them. While my daughter was growing up, we looked forward to our vacations as our special times. We would plan ahead and become excited about the activities. We would drop our change in a jar labeled 'Christmas Break' to help visualize our vacation plans taking shape. Our favorite excursion was to walk around the mall and have lunch together. You can enjoy your time together, too.

POINTERS FOR PARENTS

1. INVOLVE your children in the planning process: "What should we do?" Write down all suggestions and determine what is appropriate.

2. SCHEDULE times to visit your local library. This is free! If the family does not have library cards, this is a great time to receive one. Often, libraries schedule vacation activities: check their calendar. SCHEDULE A CERTAIN TIME OF DAY TO READ THE LIBRARY BOOKS TOGETHER AT HOME.

3. CREATE projects together: Decorating and crafting are a few suggestions.

4. INCLUDE walking and exercise time. Children have energy that needs to be burned.

5. REARRANGE their bedroom. This can be an introduction to cleaning their room. Discuss this ahead of time.

Remember: You'll have a better chance of an enjoyable and exciting vacation, if you plan ahead. Think of the time as an opportunity to spend more time with your children. Enjoy the holiday season and enjoy your children!

♦ KIDS NEED MORE LAP-TOP TIME ♦

Not the lap-top time that requires a mouse and modem . . . Not the lap-top time that costs thousands of dollars . . . Not the lap-top that requires a battery or electrical outlet. This one is free.

This **lap-top time requires a mom or dad.** This lap-top time could include a hug or kiss. Lap-top time is best when it is surrounded by a parent's loving arms and tender words. Lap-top time provides the place and the opportunity to listen, talk and console one another.

FIRST, Lap-top time is the time and the place for bonding with our children. It builds close relationships and trust. The lap-top can be the setting for many things. The lap is a secure, loving, enjoyable place to be held.

Lap-top time spells love, caring and kindness. Everyone needs that!

The bonds and relationships we create with our children last a lifetime. The words we whisper during lap-top time are special to children and parents.

Second, the all-important reading process starts in the lap. When children are very young, parents should read aloud to them. The best and most comfortable place for this reading is the lap. Studies show the parental love and caring are essential for a child's development. The same is true for the reading process. It is actually the melodic sound of the parent's voice and the security of the lap-top time that are the essential elements for success. Reading aloud with expression and rhythm begins to instill a strong love of reading.

EXAMPLE: While our daughter was growing up my husband and I always made sure we had plenty of opportunities for lap-top time. We would read her favorite books aloud with the best expression we could muster. We would vary our voices, sometimes whispering, sometimes shouting, sometimes singing. We feel it developed a closeness we still feel today. Even though our daughter lives 250 miles away, we maintain the conversations and the closeness. In addition, she became an avid reader at the age of four. She had a head start on reading when she entered kindergarten. This head start in reading helped her become an A student throughout her school years.

Still not sure of the importance of lap-top time? Imagine what our world would be like without lap-top time. What a cold, uncaring world this would be. How would we whisper "I love you" in our child's ear without lap-top time? How would we experience that closeness and security in our own lives? There would be a great void.

POINTERS FOR PARENTS

1. TAKE ADVANTAGE of the lap-top time when the children are young. They will outgrow it all too soon!
2. HOLD THE CHILDREN on your lap and whisper to them. Ask them how they are doing, and be sure to tell them you love them.
3. GRAB YOUR CHILD'S FAVORITE BOOK and read it aloud to them. Be expressive! You might even want to sing part of it.

REMEMBER: Take advantage of lap-top time while you can. Children grow up fast and we don't want to lose that window of opportunity. Lap-top time is the place and the time to bond with the children. The laptop can be the first place the child hears the sounds of reading.

♦ "IT'S *MY* ROOM!" ♦

"It's *my* bedroom . . .!" "No, it isn't and I have the mortgage payments to prove it!"

What has just happened? A parent has attempted to enter the child's bedroom, only to be reprimanded by the child. The child asserted and gained control over this situation.

If you find yourself part of a similar scenario, you have two choices: You can enter the bedroom, or you can retreat. If you enter, you assert your authority as the parent. If you retreat, it may signify that you have lost control of the child. The fact of the matter is: Parents who have lost control of their kids, have kids who are out of control.

My immediate advice to the introductory scenario is 'yes, parents do have the right to enter a child's bedroom; no question about it.' Parents not only have every right, they carry the responsibility to know what is going on behind the bedroom door.

Recently, I was counseling a parent who was mortified to learn her son was involved with drugs. The parents didn't have a clue about the drug abuse. A part of my conversation with the parents went something like this:

Dr. Kennedy: ". . . And so, what posters are on your child's bedroom wall?"

Parent: "I don't know, I never go in there . . . I'm not allowed."

Dr. Kennedy: "Why do you think you are not allowed?"

Parent: "My son told me I couldn't go in there."

STOP RIGHT THERE! I didn't need to inquire any further.

The obvious problem was that the parents were no longer in control. The second problem was that the teenager was running their lives. I suggested they enter their child's room and examine the decorations and wall decor.

Later that same day, they went into their son's bedroom. Glancing at the poster-filled walls, they quickly determined there were life-size pictures of drug-using musicians. The song lyrics were written on the poster, lauding the drug euphoria.

The clues to the drug abuse were right there under the parent's roof.

The posters on any child's wall shout out: "This is who I am… This is what's important to me." Most often, the musical choice goes hand in hand with the choice of posters.

POINTERS FOR PARENTS

1. CLAIM or reclaim your parental rights to the children's bedrooms.
2. ANNOUNCE to the family that you will be visiting bedrooms; it is a parental responsibility.
3. CONSIDER PRIVACY: Consider there may be short periods of time when your child may need privacy. But this never supersedes your authority or responsibility to be aware of what is going on in that room. Common sense is needed here.

REMEMBER: It's a parent's responsibility to monitor and be aware of what is in the bedroom and what is going on in that bedroom. Know what posters decorate the walls and who the people are in the posters.

♦ THAT NEIGHBORHOOD FEELING ♦

During a recent Hurricane Georges evacuation I was reminded of the need and value of neighborhoods. There's that feeling of being together and leaning on one another. There's the comfort of just seeing one another and talking with one another, alleviating the anxieties.

Preparing to evacuate is an anxious time but it was the neighbors who provided the calming effect. Think about this: You are going to evacuate and have a matter of hours to decide what exactly are your valuables and what you will lose, should your home take a direct hit from the hurricane. You know how large your vehicle is and you know it won't hold many bulky items. So many questions . . . So few answers.

We had our 'hurricane evac' list, but had limited time. My husband and I walked outside just to see what the other neighbors were doing. They were meandering around chatting with one another. Neighbors were staring at the darkened, cloudy sky first, then surveying the murky tidal river, already at its crest. What should we do first? Or, is it a false warning? Maybe it won't hit us.

Conversations similar to the following could be heard throughout the neighborhood:

Neighbor 1: "What are you doing to prepare? Are you staying here or evacuating?"

Neighbor 2: "I don't know, I keep listening to the weatherman; we'll decide soon."

Neighbor 3: "My husband bought the plywood, but hasn't decided if he should put it up yet."

Neighbor 4: "My husband just returned from the lumberyard and they are out of plywood . . . oh no, what will we do now?"

Neighbor 2: "Don't worry, I think we have a few extra pieces of plywood –you can have those . . ."

Neighbor 1: "We ended up with two extras . . .you can have those, too . . .how many total do you need?"

Neighbor 4: "Oh thank you so much, I don't know what I'd do without you neighbors!"

Neighbor 1: "How much water do you have? And don't forget your insurance papers, checkbooks and get some cash . . .if the power goes, so do the ATMs . . . and don't forget those pictures—you can't replace those old pictures of the family . . ."

Neighbor 2: "Thanks for the reminder—I have only $40.00, and I have to find all those old pictures . . . I have a lot to do . . ."

And on and on it went—from anxiety-ridden worry to cooperative calm. I felt an immense sense of relief and, at the same time, energized and focused to do what I knew needed to be done!

I felt so much better, just knowing we were all in the same situation. I guess we were doing all the right things, we just forgot a few of them. The important thing: All the neighbors forgot *different* things and so we all helped each other in the preparation.

Next came the plywood. Later that afternoon it was time to decide if we should really attach that heavy, floppy wood to the concrete block stucco. It's a lot of work, and maybe the hurricane will miss us.

Suddenly a neighbor begins the arduous task of sawing all the sheets of plywood to match each window size! We didn't count on spending all those hours fitting each one to a specific window. Quickly, we decide to drill the holes in our stucco home for the plywood, without the exact measurement. The neighbor across the street opted to evacuate and merely tape the windows in the crisscross fashion. The neighbor down the street begins to saw. The buzzing of drills and saws echoes throughout this once-quiet neighborhood.

Neighbors began to assist one another with the plywood, as it was almost too cumbersome for one individual to handle. Then, anxious looks transformed to faint smiles, as the plywood pounding continued through the darkened, cloudy afternoon. Thank God for this neighborhood.

The meteorologist announces: "Okay, it's time to take this storm seriously . . . it looks like it could hit us directly."

That provided the final surge of adrenaline! Plywood covered all the windows. Now, we had to bring all loose objects into the house or garage. Ugh—we thought we were done. Momentarily, as if to read my mind, the teenage neighbor ran over to ask if we needed help. My husband, as always, was about to utter 'oh no'—but I interrupted him in mid-stream and exclaimed —'Oh yes, thank you!'

Finally, we load all our valuables and personal belongings that would fit into the car. The back seat was stacked to the car ceiling. I utter a last thought: Shouldn't we take our computer? It has all my business files on it . . . My husband groans with exhaustion . . .

One last look—what else should we take, just in case this house is blown away?

We secure the cat in the laundry room/garage. I hated to leave her—but didn't have any choice on that one . . .

Our plan is to evacuate to our daughter's place in Central Florida. Suddenly, I recall, I told her several hours ago we would leave 'shortly.' The phone rings—it's our daughter: "Ma, you haven't left yet? What's taking so long? Are you all right?"

We relay all we have done in preparation, and decide we will leave within the hour, before the highways are jammed and bumper to bumper. I try to fight the lump in my throat, thinking of the seriousness of the entire situation.

Within an hour we appear to be ready. We load the final box into the already stuffed car. We look next door to Mary's house. She's an elderly widow and has just entered her driveway. We thought she had already evacuated, as no one was around. We learn that she has decided to stay. She surveys the neighborhood to see all the boarded-up windows. Worry envelops her and she says: 'Uh, oh, I don't have any plywood.' Within minutes, my husband notifies the other neighbors: 'Hey, she doesn't have any plywood, anybody have any extra?'

Immediately, he retrieved a piece from our garage, and two other neighbors did the same. The guys went into action again—and proceeded to drill and mount Mary's plywood over the windows. It didn't take long—she was so grateful and said: "Oh, thank you, I don't know what I'd do without you neighbors."

At this point we are completely exhausted and just want to stay in our house, in our neighborhood to be sure everyone is okay. My thoughts are interrupted by the loud ringing of our phone.

I run into the house. The caller, worried, inquires:

"Mom, I can't believe you guys are still there. I thought you were leaving two hours ago. Are you okay?

What's taking you so long?"

"Now, we're ready, just had to help our neighbor."

And so, to our daughter's we went. Thank God, Hurricane Georges did not hit Florida. We experienced only heavy rain.

I sincerely hope the panhandle of Florida, Alabama and Louisiana had neighbors as special and helpful as mine.

♦ JUST SAY NO! ♦

The child who never *hears* 'no' does not know how to *say* 'no.' Parents are not doing children any favors by continually saying 'yes' to their demands. When parents provide the no's with the yes's, children are aware of their boundaries. If parents do not set the limits, children will discover boundaries from their peers or the television. If we include the no's with the yes's we begin to train children in the proper method to make choices in life.

Children are small adults in training. Parents are the trainers. If we are to train our children to be productive adults we need to show them how to discern between right and wrong. A common myth is: "If I say yes all the time to my children, then they will love me more." The answer to this myth is NO, NO, NO! If parents say yes all the time, children often feel this person cares little about their actions. Children need and want boundaries. They respond favorably as guidelines are established.

When parents say 'no' with the 'yes,' they are creating the choice-making ability in children. When boundaries are set, children begin to discern right and wrong, good and bad. It's no secret that life is a series of choices. If we give our children the tools to make intelligent choices, they will be able to choose what is right for a particular situation.

The training parents provide in the home *sets the stage* for the arena of life. The relationship parents build with children will be the relationship children expect from other adults.

For example: If children are accustomed to creating their own sets of rules, they will have difficulty wherever there are rules. Rules are everywhere. All of us have been to school. When children refuse to follow school rules, they end up in internal suspensions, timeouts, and out-of-school suspensions.

POINTERS FOR PARENTS

HINT: Be ready for an argument or rebellion from the children if you are not used to saying ' no.'

If you aren't used to *saying* 'no,' they are certainly not used to *hearing* 'no.' Be patient and persevere: It will take time. It will pay off!

1. NO WITH THE YES: Begin to say in situations: "No, you cannot do this, but you can do this . . ." This begins to set clear behavior parameters.

2. TV TIME: Set limits on the amount and type of television viewing. Allow children 30-60 minutes /day during the week and 1-2 hours/day on the weekend. Use your common sense and know what they are watching. When children are watching television, they are doing little else. They are not reading, socializing or exercising.

3. TELEPHONE LINES: When parents agree to a separate phone line for the children, parents agree to surrender control of the telephone. Parents have in effect said: "You can talk to whomever you want and whenever you want." As the teen years bring additional phone calls, set ground rules. For example: "No phone calls after nine p.m. If you receive calls prior to that time, limit the call to ten minutes." Consider call waiting instead of a separate line. That will give you the control back and the child some freedom with the calls, with the responsibility of stopping when they hear the beep of an incoming call.

4. APPROPRIATE DRESS: Begin assisting when children are young. We all know teens feel a need to dress as they

please. However, parents still have the right and responsibility to set limits. For example: “When you wear a skirt, hold your arms to your sides, and where the fingertips hit, that is the shortest the skirt should be.” Notice you have included the positive as well as the negative with providing direction. Many schools are imposing ‘uniform’ dress to avoid dealing with this complex issue.

REMEMBER: When parents say ‘no,’ they also say ‘yes’ to what children can do. For example: “No, you cannot watch TV all day; yes, you can watch TV for one hour.” When parents take the initiative to say no, their children will then be able to know how to say no as choices confront them throughout life. Parents will do the right thing when they choose between yes and no.

♦...OH PURPLE MOUNTAIN MAJESTIES...♦

Having just returned from a vacation in Colorado, many visions and memories continue to dance around in my mind ... Pikes Peak, The Royal Gorge, and Garden of the Gods. The most vivid picture is found in the song “America the Beautiful”: “Oh purple mountain majesties . . .” That phrase is describing Pikes Peak at sunrise and sunset! The mountain is actually a deep purple color! The trip was awe-inspiring as well as educational. The scenery, the history and formation of the mountains and surrounding vistas made a lasting impression upon me. I’ve heard people say, “If you haven’t seen the Rockies, you haven’t really seen this great country of ours. The sights are breathtaking! Now I completely understand this message.

I never realized that when Katharine Lee Bates penned the great patriotic song, “America the Beautiful” in 1904, she was sitting atop Pikes Peak. Once my husband and I completed the 14,110-foot climb up Pikes Peak, "America the Beautiful" took on a brand new meaning for us. Let me clarify—my husband and I did not *climb the peak*, we *drove the trek*, which was frightening enough! And may I add—there were no guardrails, and I feared we were going to fall right over the side and never be heard from or seen again. Luckily, I was wrong and we reached the summit to see all its splendid glory! We witnessed first-hand the "purple mountain majesties above the fruited plain." We envisioned the "amber waves of grain" in the plains below.

I felt a part of the inspiration Katharine Lee Bates must have felt: There is nothing like being nearly three miles above sea level, *staring down* at the tree line. That's another interesting fact I was reminded of: Trees don't grow above 12,000 feet!

I touched the icy, old snow, juxtaposed alongside the shimmering red and yellow wildflowers. The scene exemplified all the contrasting elements of life below 14,110 feet. The winds were so strong, it was difficult to stand upright, as the fear mingled with excitement at Pikes Peak summit.

There's something powerful about looking down at the world. To curb my fear, I kept repeating to myself: "I know I am 14,110 feet closer to God, should anything happen to me. . .I'll just get to heaven faster." My fear and hesitations then quickly were transformed into jubilation and excitement.

I couldn't believe I was there—on top of Pikes Peak, a place I had only heard about in years past. The song "America the Beautiful" continued to ring in my ears.

And that is my parenting advice today: Tell your children about our great country. Show them pictures, and if possible, travel to a place you have not visited. You don't have to go to Pikes Peak to show them the grandeur; there are many sights closer to you.

Let's reclaim our patriotism and respect for our country. This past Fourth of July rekindled my love and appreciation for these United States. The Fourth of July may be over for now, but there are many more to come. And our country has 222 years of rich history we can explore.

While vacationing over this Fourth of July, I witnessed many Independence Day celebrations. One that particularly impressed me was a reading of the "Declaration of Independence" in the Garden of the Gods.

Too often children think the Fourth of July simply means another day for a picnic or a vacation from summer school. The more our children know about America, the more they will respect it and carry on its traditions.

POINTERS FOR PARENTS

1. GET A COPY of the "Declaration of Independence" and read it with your children. This can be a great beginning to many more activities.
2. FIND A COPY of "America the Beautiful": Examine the words and sing it together.
3. RESEARCH THE SIGNERS of the Declaration: Who were they? What were they like? What did they do for a living? Compare and contrast it to leaders of today.
4. STUDY JULY 4TH: What happened? What events led up to that day? This could inspire numerous topics for fun and discussion. It would be fun to dress up as the characters did over 200 years ago.
5. RELY ON YOUR LIBRARY or school for information.
6. TELL your librarian you want *reliable* information.
7. BE AWARE that some newly printed history books may not be 100% accurate. You may be better off requesting older material.

REMEMBER: It is our duty as parents to learn about this great country, the United States. Once we know and appreciate its greatness, we then gladly pass it along to our children.

♦ EVERYONE LIKES A ROUTINE ♦

Getting in a rut isn't all bad! It is rather comforting to know what's going to happen, when it's going to happen and for how long. People seem to need a routine in order to get things accomplished.

A routine builds structure and purpose in our daily lives. Once a particular routine is set, people become accustomed to it. If the routine should change one could feel disturbed and out of sorts. Most adults and children seem to appreciate the security of a routine.

To develop a routine in our day is actually the organization of it. When particular activity is scheduled for a particular day or time of day, there is a greater probability the action will occur.

The sense of commitment and accomplishment can be built into our home and work lives. Did you ever notice when you write it down it gets done—either in your Day Timer or on the sticky note on your kitchen table? As soon as you complete the task cross it off or write a check by it. That's a great feeling of satisfaction!

Try building a routine with the children in the home. If children know what to expect at a certain time of day, they will look forward to it and be prepared for it. This technique will be effective in various activities. Routines can be established for bed times and bath times. Choose one routine and stick to it. Children like routines so much that if parents change it, they express disapproval.

POINTERS FOR PARENTS

1. DECIDE on a bedtime. Make it early enough so the children get enough sleep for school the next day.

2. CHOOSE a particular time to read for 30 minutes with your child. Early evening or shortly after school is a good time.

3. CHOOSE a special time to have a snack with the children right after school. It doesn't have to be expensive; graham crackers and a beverage are a few suggestions.

4. RELAX and (each) talk about their day at the same time you're eating the snack. The snack will set the right tone for talking.

5. TELL the children about the set times so they will look forward to the routine.

REMEMBER: Everyone likes a routine. Build a schedule at home with the children and you'll be amazed how much you will accomplish. If the routine is changed or broken, be sure to communicate to the children the reason for the change. The children will look forward to the routine.

♦ R-E-S-P-E-C-T ♦

As a parent, one of the singular, most important things to teach our children is RESPECT. Respect is the key to success in many aspects of life. Respect is the thread that holds together friendships and relationships of all kinds. Respect is not a new notion by any means. Rather, it is a necessary atmosphere that needs to be in the forefront of parenting. It will set the stage for the entire development of the child.

Webster's Dictionary defines respect as: "high admiration, polite regard or consideration." Respect is a learned behavior. Children learn to be respectful or disrespectful very early in life. The first four to five years are the most formative in a child's life. The child learns respect by watching and listening to the parents.

The way a child treats his/her parents is the way the child will treat all other authority figures in life.

How does a busy parent begin to teach respect? For starters, remember, EVERYTHING WE DO COUNTS!

POINTERS FOR PARENTS

1. REALIZE you, the parent, are the key! The 'power is with you.
2. EXHIBIT respectful behaviors in the home. Set a good example with your spouse. You are the child's first teacher and role model.
3. TELL your children what respect is: "Respect is important; be considerate and polite to others."
4. BEGIN by incorporating respectful phrases: Please, thank you and I'm sorry.
5. EMPHASIZE the importance of others and their feelings. Use examples in the home or the world around you.

REMEMBER: The parent is the child's first teacher. If the parent teaches respect to the child, the child will treat the parent respectfully. The way a child treats his parents is the way he/she will treat other authority figures.

♦ TIME TO REFLECT ♦

As a new year approaches it's time to reflect on our parenting over the past year. What grade would we give ourselves? What were our strengths and weaknesses? How can we improve?

No matter how great a parent we are, there must be one or two areas upon which we can improve. Think about the great moments when you knew you did the right thing with your family. Those were special. Then think about the times when you said: "Oh, oh, I shouldn't have done that . . .or I'll never do that again."

What were the 'should haves or nevers?' Make a mental note or a real note to see how your family can be even better.

Check out the following areas or write down concerns of your own.

POINTERS FOR PARENTS

1. TELEVISION TIME: Ask: How much time do my kids sit in front of the television? For the most part, TV time is unproductive, idle time for children. Consider limiting TV time to 30-60 minutes per day. That creates time for activities such as reading or physical activity.

2. COMMUNICATION: It should be a priority to show concern for family members. Ask about their day. Ask specific questions to show you are genuinely interested in the children's activities.

EXAMPLE:
Parent: How was school?
Child: Uh, okay.
Parent: What do you mean, okay? What did you learn in English or math? (Pick your own topic here.)
Child: Let's see, we learned about prefixes and suffixes, and stuff.
Parent: Tell me about prefixes and suffixes . . . I'm not sure what you mean. Do you have any handouts or homework?
Child: I have a handout I can show you.
And so on . . .

The idea is to be specific and ask about a particular teacher, class or subject. Many parents just accept the 'uh, okays' and don't continue the conversations.

If you usually do not pursue a subject with the kids, they will be a bit surprised at this new approach, but they'll like it. They'll be glad you really want information about their day.

3. REWARD GOOD DEEDS. Find something good about each family member. Be sure to brag to everyone about the successes of each member. A good time for bragging is dinner time when everyone is together.

4. DINNER TIME: This is more than just a time to eat. This is a special time to communicate: Talk, laugh and tell each other about the day. Choose a meal that is ideal for your family. Ask: which meal is the best time for all to be together? I know families who never sit down and eat together. This could be a sign of lost communication and dwindling concern. Choose a time, tell everyone and follow through with this activity.

5. FAMILY READING TIME: Once you reduce TV time, there will be more time for reading. Families that read together are better readers. When parents participate, the kids know the importance of reading. Visit the library together and choose special times in the family when everyone reads. Read aloud and silently. Parents should read aloud first. Don't force the children to read aloud; wait until they volunteer. If they never volunteer, ask why. If you feel there may be a reading problem, call the school and ask about your child's reading level.

REMEMBER: No one's perfect. Choose one or two areas to become an even better parent. You'll be glad you did!

♦ SPORTS AND PARENTING ♦

We can learn many lessons of life from the world of sports. Our favorite sports activity or broadcast can be transformed to an arena displaying appropriate and inappropriate behavior. Of course, as the spectator we certainly can enjoy the game and scream for our favorite team and player. As a parent and teacher I never miss an opportunity to use that teachable moment . . .even if it's on a football field.

We can use the sports arena for good examples and bad examples. If we want to make our parenting point relevant to our sports-minded children, we need to become a spectator and join in the fun!

The following values can be observed in the sports arena and incorporated into our potpourri of parenting.

POINTERS FOR PARENTS
You can apply this to any sport.

SPORTS CAN HELP US TEACH:

- RESPECT FOR AUTHORITY: The players need to respect decisions made by the referees. In life, we may not always like the decisions made by those in authority, but we must abide by them. To argue with a referee is wrong and should be used as an example of inappropriate behavior.
- COOPERATION: Cooperation is needed on the team and in life. Players who play as a team have a much better chance of winning.
- PRACTICE, PRACTICE, PRACTICE: Hours of practice precede each game. Players do not merely walk on the

field without practicing. The skill of reading requires practice to ensure progress and success.

- LEARN FROM OUR MISTAKES: We all make mistakes and it is best if we can learn from them.
- LOSING AND WINNING: It's best to be a gracious and grateful winner. It's tougher to lose. However, losing can show us our shortcomings and the best way to improve.
- ENTERTAINMENT: Sports of any kind can provide family entertainment. And if the game is televised, it is virtually free. If your family is on a budget the televised sports can be a starting point for family gatherings, including discussions and food!
- ROLE MODEL: Whether we like it or not, sports figures are perceived by children as role models. As parents, we communicate to our children the parameters of good behavior. FOR EXAMPLE: If your child's favorite basketball player dyes his hair orange, you need to tell them it is inappropriate and harmful. Secondly, if their favorite baseball player has just admitted to drug abuse, parents must emphasize the illegality of this behavior. Parents need to say this behavior is wrong even though the favorite player is the guilty party. Encourage choice of a new role model.

ON A POSITIVE NOTE: Applaud the courage and humility of recent sports heroes such as Sammy Sosa and Mark McGwire. We were starving for a worthy hero to model good behavior and we received two!

REMEMBER: Be creative and enjoy your parenting. By utilizing sports heroes and games as the 'idea box' for parenting, our teachings may have a more lasting effect on the children.

♦ SPRING HAS SPRUNG! ♦

The weather is warmer . . . The air is softer . . . The days are longer . . . Barbecue aromas fill the moist air . . . Lightheartedness and laughter spill into the day.

The kids are sillier. They have even more energy than normal. It's hard for everyone to concentrate . . .the mind wanders . . .

Don't panic! It's only spring! With spring comes a spring break for some or long weekends for others. Some of us continue to work outside the home. Others may have a spring break or vacation time. Concerns may be raised if the children are home and we are not. Or, we wonder what we will do with them and all that extra energy they seem to have this time of year.

Sometimes it seems parents are the ultimate jugglers of time and energy. We can take advantage of the children's extra energy and channel it into positive activities. We can't fight that extra burst of spring energy, so we might as well make the best of it. We can PLAN, PARTICIPATE AND PLAY TOGETHER.

Spring and vacations can be the best of times. When my daughter was growing up, I regarded our weekends and vacations as special times to spend more time together. We would plan our day to sleep in, shop, create craft projects and even to organize her room! We looked forward to the times when she didn't have to go to school and I didn't have to go to work. We saved our money for those special times. Then we wouldn't feel guilty about going to the mall and spending a little extra money. Those were great times! She's now a young adult, and we still enjoy spending time together, sometimes just talking over a cup of coffee.

Once you start the tradition of planning and playing together, it can carry into adulthood. When your children become adults, and trust me, they will, you'll enjoy each other's company. As parents, we set the stage when they are young.

POINTERS FOR PARENTS

1. PLAN ACTIVITIES and projects together. If possible, plan ahead so you can buy any materials you may need. Don't begin the activity until the vacation or weekend begins. You want the time to be special.
2. PLAN SPECIAL snack items and times. Set the time aside. Be sure to tell the children the time you expect them to join you for the snack. Maybe a picnic in the backyard . . .
3. SCHEDULE a day to visit the library. If you need library cards, now is the perfect time to get one. Check out books together. Read to each other when you arrive home.
4. CHOOSE ONE DAY to clean the bedrooms. That means your bedroom and theirs. Then they will feel part of an important activity. Take them step by step in the room-cleaning process. Help in the organization process. As you are cleaning your bedroom, explain to them what you are doing.

REMEMBER: Be positive. Plan, participate, and play together. Enjoy the children when they are home. You're building a relationship that will last a lifetime.

♦ Summer Fun! ♦

Let's look at the bright side. Summertime can be a fun time for children and parents. It goes without saying that even though parenting is one of the toughest jobs we will ever have; it is also one of the most rewarding and enjoyable. Parenting has its ups and downs, but what job doesn't? Once we have accepted this position, we do the best we can, and have fun in the process.

As we approach the *lazy, hazy, crazy* days of summer, we can begin to create a positive mind-set of summer planning. If it seems we've run out of ideas and don't know what to do this summer, we open up the discussions for the entire family.

Here are some suggestions to begin to create summer fun. Read these suggestions aloud to your family and ask for their feedback. They will feel they have a part in the planning and begin to have positive thoughts about summertime.

POINTERS FOR PARENTS

1. IDEA JAR OR BOX: Find an old jar or shoe box. Ask for family volunteers to decorate it and place it in an area for all to see. Invite all to write suggestions for family activities. Read them aloud at the dinner table or early evening when everyone is together. To keep it interesting, change the jar or box every few weeks. Decide who will get to keep the 'old jar' in their room. If it's 'family made' do not throw it away. Remember, as the parent you do have the ultimate veto power and can weed out the impossible suggestions that may be made.

2. PLAN ACTIVE FUN TIMES and *quieter inactive* times. Believe it or not, kids do enjoy the quiet sometimes, just as parents do. The parent needs to initiate this idea. Children

certainly will not admit they enjoy quiet times; not at first, anyway.

3. EDUCATIONAL OPPORTUNITES: We want to keep their brains active as well as their bodies. What subjects or areas of interest would be beneficial to your family? When our daughter was growing up we concentrated on reading, math and geography in the summer months. If you don't have a clue on this one, call the school and ask for suggestions. They usually have some great summer fun ideas, while sneaking in some learning at the same time.

4. GEOGRAPHY: We are AAA members and would always call the nearest office to receive their old tour books and expired maps. With the tour books and maps we would plan a real or imaginary trip. We automatically included reading and math skills while planning the trip and it was great fun for our family. Children can create collages with all the pictures and maps from the books. They can then decorate their rooms with the finished products. Even if you are not AAA members, still call them to see if they have any expired tour books you could have. The books are usually only a few months old.

4. HINT: Last year, when I attempted to teach a map reading unit to middle school students, I was shocked that only about 10% knew the directions: north, south, east, west and the combinations. The educational staff of AAA and I planned the unit together and we had to back up to the basics. Simply draw the directions (north, south, east and west) on paper and show the children what they mean. Then ask them to draw it for you, as a type of quiz. Once they have mastered the directions, you can move on to the trip planning.

5. DIRECTION in your neighborhood: Once you have instilled the north, south, east, west skill, apply it to your home, neighborhood and town. Discuss the directions of the roads in your area. Discuss your home, and which way is north, south,

east or west. This activity can lead to many other activities, limited only by your imagination . . .

REMEMBER: As parents we set the tone in our household. Look at the bright side—summertime can be fun time. Incorporate both noisy *and quiet* activities to carry you through the hot summer months. Your family will begin to look forward to the times you will be together. ENJOY!

♦ JUST SETTLING IN ♦

AAHHH . . . THE KIDS HAVE BEEN BACK TO SCHOOL for some time now and things seem to have settled in . . . The anxieties have diminished . . . No more questions about the dress code . . . No more worries . . .

HOLD THAT THOUGHT! WISH IT WERE SO . . .

Let's enjoy that settled in feeling for a while longer, keeping in mind, there are more new and exciting challenges right around the corner.

Okay, time's up!

Now that we're settled in, the key is how to keep it or repeat it. Parents can use that time to catch up, be informed or prepare for upcoming events. If the kids are already a few weeks or months into school, then so are the grades, homework and school friendships.

By now you have probably already decorated your refrigerator with lunch menus and other attractive handouts. Perhaps school lunches we could do without, but what about those *other* handouts? Do they have important dates on them? Did I read them?

POINTERS FOR PARENTS

ACADEMIC MATTERS

1. REPORT CARD DATES: What are they? Mark *your* calendars as children often tend to 'lose' their report cards from school to home.

2. INTERIM REPORTS: Interim reports are sent home midway between report card times, if your school uses them. If your school has nine-week grading periods, then your child should receive the interims the fourth week of that period. Ask school officials if all the children receive interims or just the failing students.

3. PTO MEETINGS: Does your school have these? Where? When? Mark your calendar.

SOCIAL MATTERS

1. KNOW your children's friends and everything about them: their names, their appearance, their parents, their grades and their hobbies. Yes, it's your business and your responsibility.

2. ASK the children if they like school and why or why not. This can lead to numerous topics, limited only by time!

3. HOW do they seem to get along with other children and adults? Find out the name of their best friend and favorite teacher. Who is the least-liked teacher? Be sure to probe until you get an answer. If you suspect your child is being mimicked or mistreated at school, do not hesitate to call and follow through on this.

EXTRACURRICULAR ACTIVITIES

These are **extra** *activities your child may take on if they can handle the regular classwork and responsibilities. They may be before or after school.*

1. LEARN what the activities are and decide if your child has the time and energy to get involved.
2. IF YOU DECIDE to pursue one of these after-school activities, monitor your child's involvement. Often, these become the 'only curricular' activities and grades may begin to drop.

REMEMBER: If you like that settled-in feeling, the real key is to keep it or repeat it. Take advantage of those slower times to plan ahead and pace your parenting throughout the year. That settled-in feeling is good. It means you've done a good job—you've earned it!

♦ "THANK YOU!" ♦

How many times have you spent your hard-earned money at a store, only to end up with the cashier's blank stare? The change is dropped in your hand, swimming in the crumpled receipt. You didn't see a grateful smile; you didn't hear the expected 'thank you.'

When this happens to me, I feel cheated and frustrated at the same time. I feel as though the sale wasn't entirely completed, and there is something missing. Occasionally, I get infuriated, depending upon the intensity of the cold stare from the cashier. My reaction will depend upon the severity of the rude behavior and my level of energy at the time of sale. I'll ask myself: Do I want to change this behavior or not? Is it worth the additional frustration the conversation will produce?

At times, I just want to scream: "How dare you not even say thank you, after I just handed over $125.00 of my hard-earned money!" Other times, I want to pass it off as ignorance. Usually, the *teacher in me* insists on coming out. This can be a very teachable moment.

Let me share some of my teachable moments: After the receipt is thrust in my palm and no thank you is uttered I'll say: "Excuse me, what did you say?" They look at me as though I'm from another planet. The cashier now emits a condescending glare. I'll repeat: "Pardon me?" Their stare is colder now. And I'll conclude: "Oh, you said *thank you!* Well, *you're welcome!"*

They'll go back to their computerized cash register, in a fog about this entire exchange. A large percentage of the youngsters don't even have a clue about what just occurred. Occasionally, my husband and I will wait until we hear the long-awaited 'thank you.' We make that decision based on the number of people in line and the amount of time we have to devote to this moment.

Perhaps the young person doesn't intend to be impolite or rude, but that is the impression they give to the other person. And that is the crucial point: to show that we care and act accordingly. Somewhere along the line of growing up, many children have missed the importance of manners in our culture.

As a teenager, I worked those summer jobs of clerk and salesperson. As I recall, thank you was an expected response. I'm quite sure we were trained by the department store, and if we did not act properly, we were notified pronto.

The obvious question is: What happened?

To begin with, it is our job as parents to see that manners and polite behavior are instilled at home. This is the place where it all begins. We set the foundation for behavior.

Relatives, extended families, neighbors and communities in which we live should *reinforce* and *expect* proper behavior.

How can we begin to teach our children to say thank you? IT IS NOT DIFFICULT—IT JUST NEEDS TO BE A PART OF OUR PARENTING PACKAGE.

POINTERS FOR PARENTS

1. ROLE MODEL: Be a positive role model for the children. Make a point to include *please* and *thank you* in the conversations with your spouse. Children need to see and hear the proper methods of interaction.
2. COMMUNICATE this expectation to the children when they are very young. As a mom or dad, you can begin saying *please* and *thank you* when children are infants. Then these words will become a natural part of the child's language.
3. SING: Make up songs with the *two words* in them. Create a contest with the family and sing the songs around the house. This can really be fun. Choose a tune you like and start from there.
4. REWARD: When your children incorporate *please* and *thank you* into their language give them a hug and kiss to let them know how important that behavior is to you. Make a point at the dinner table to laud the good behavior. The other children will quickly follow suit. If children know this is important to you, and you recognize it when they 'do it right,' that is motivation enough for them.

REMEMBER: If we instill polite behavior at home, our children will become role models for other children. Other children will see the positive feedback your children are getting and will follow suit. AND SO, <u>PLEASE</u> HAVE A GOOD DAY, AND <u>THANK YOU</u> FOR MAKING THE EFFORT TO DO IT RIGHT IN YOUR HOUSE!

♦ TAKE THE TIME ♦

"HURRY, HURRY, HURRY. I never have time for anything! Where does all my time go? It seems all I do is get up, go to work, get tired, watch TV and collapse into bed!"

Do you ever catch yourself saying that? Do you ever feel so busy you can't see straight? It seems we are so caught up in the hustle and bustle we don't even notice the precious things around us.

That scenario has a familiar ring to me. Mine went something like this: Up at 5:30, get my daughter ready, drop her off at daycare, rush to work, pick her up at daycare, race home, make dinner, throw the dishes in the sink, run to little league, be team-mother at the game, trek home, prepare for bed, read a story and then . . . pass out from exhaustion.

I was wired, but always tired. I knew I had to make some changes.

Children often yell: "Mom, Dad, let's play ball!"
Parents reply: "I can't, I don't have time."

STOP RIGHT THERE! SLOW DOWN AND TAKE THE TIME! We have the time; we have to take the time. When our lives are so busy we tell our own kids we don't have time, we have a problem.

IT'S TIME TO READJUST. Family and children need to be at the top of our priority list, not at the bottom. They deserve the right amount of time, not what's left over.

We all have the same amount of time every day: 24 hours. It's what we do with it that matters. And what we do with it reveals our priorities.

WHAT ARE MY PRIORITIES?

Ask this question: *What is most important to me?* Then follow it up with: *What is least important to me?* Some people find these questions difficult to answer. You may need to give this some thought. Whatever answer you supply should correspond with the way you spend your day.

IF I NEED TO READJUST MY PRIORITIES, WHERE DO I START?

POINTERS FOR PARENTS

1. FIRST, map out your day to determine *how* you spend your time. ASK yourself: How do I spend my time?
2. NEXT, write down your priorities. ASK: What is most important to me?
3. EXAMINE your answer to numbers one and two above. If you discover your top priorities are not getting most of your time, you've identified a problem.
4. If the kids are not on the top of the PRIORITY LIST, *they should be.*

NOW READJUST . . .

5. Once you've moved the kids and family to the top of the list, other adjustments are necessary. If you've moved something up, some other priority moves down.

FOR EXAMPLE: A co-worker's priority list looked like this: 1. Work 2. Cleaning 3. Children 4. Cooking

To move the kids to the number-one slot, she had to *readjust* her priorities. She decided a clean house would have to become *less* of a priority than spending time with her children. She made the right decision. Her new priorities became: 1-Children, 2-Work, 3-Cleaning, 4-Cooking.

THE FACT IS: OUR KIDS WOULD RATHER HAVE US THAN A SPARKLING CLEAN HOUSE.

REMEMBER: We all have the same amount of time each day. We have the time; we just need to take the time. If you have discovered that your kids are not number one on your priority list, readjust. What our kids really want most is more time with us. Enjoy!

♦ WHERE DOES ALL MY TIME GO? ♦

Where does all my time go? I had good intentions, but it seems nothing was really accomplished today. . .I don't get it, what happened?

Ever find yourself saying that? I have, and if I don't remember a few basic rules, I find myself still repeating those words.

Some reminders: If I don't write it down, it doesn't get done. If I don't actually schedule certain activities they don't get done either.

This applies whether you are a stay-at-home mom, an employee outside of the home or operate a home business.

I've been confronted with this issue of time management since I started my own consulting business, operating from the home.

There's the issue of all my time is mine and I can do what I want mind-set. That led me to write down what I would accomplish each day for the business. I had to carry that one step further and manage my home time to avoid interference with my business time.

It seemed more complicated because I had business time and home time overlapping. If you are in a similar situation, you need to manage your business time and learn to separate it from the home time.

For starters, I had to write down all my business appointments and home tasks for each day. I wrote these appointments down the day before to ready my mind-set for the next business day. Then I wrote a separate list for my home tasks and the time of day I would work on them. EXAMPLE: Monday morning: 1. Pay bills 2. Do one load of laundry. 3. Enter my business office by 9:00 a.m.

I discovered that if I neglected to write down what and when to do home or business tasks, nothing was accomplished and frustration set in.

Time managed me. I needed to be the one managing my own time.

Now when I have completed a task, I grasp my red pen and scratch out the task. This effort gives me a great sense of accomplishment whether the task was business or home related. Then when someone asks me, "So what did you do today?" I have an easy reference.

POINTERS FOR PARENTS

Apply to your individual circumstance: home or work

1. ASK AND ANSWER: Where does all my time go? Write your answer down, so you can actually see where it goes.
2. EVALUATE your individual situation: Are there certain times of the day which are best for certain events? EXAMPLE: I discovered that I was most successful if I

completed a few home tasks right away, then retreated to my office to begin my consulting for the day.

3. Once you've evaluated your own situation, write down what you WANT TO ACCOMPLISH tomorrow. Indicate if it is morning, afternoon or evening. With my own business, I've discovered it is sometimes more productive to work into the evening.

4. SCHEDULE TASKS AND ACTIVITIES. EXAMPLE: If there's a family event that always gets put on the back burner and you really want it accomplished, discuss it with the family, schedule it and write it down. Then it will get done.

REMEMBER: If you write it down, it will get done. You'll be happy when you are the manager of your time.

♦ FAMILY TRADITIONS ♦

Tradition is the foundation upon which the present is built. Tradition is the vehicle transporting values and priorities. We can think about traditions on a national level or on a very personal level. At the national level we have the tradition of singing the "Star Spangled Banner" before a sports event. We also have our Independence Day, Fourth of July, which sets the U.S. apart as a free nation. These traditions contributed to the solid foundation of our country. On the personal level, families have traditions which build strong, solid families.

Traditions paint a picture of who we are and what we represent. Lately, I've been hearing too much about the unimportance and frivolity of tradition. The chant for change rings in my ears! I hear it in the schools, neighborhoods, churches, on television and on the radio.

I ASK: Is the change better than what we have? Why should we surrender that tradition? Most of the time, 'the change agent' cannot answer that question. That is when I chant: BEWARE . . .

AN EXAMPLE many of us can identify with is the resounding result of eliminating phonics from reading programs during the 1980s. Anyone who has experienced the reading process knows that phonics is the foundation to reading success. Before we can move to other skill areas we need to learn letter sounds and word-attack skills in reading. The chant of the 1980s was 'let's just teach *whole word,* then the students won't need to learn each individual sound.'

As a reading specialist I saw a great number of middle and high school students who were unable to pronounce words and comprehend selections. Thousands of children were cheated out of a sound reading foundation because someone said 'let's change, let's do it a new way.' Schools now realize the mistake and are attempting to rectify it. Parents want the traditional foundation of phonics back in the schools. There was a good reason for phonics: IT WORKED!

In the same sense, family traditions make a statement: This is what makes us unique; this is important to us; this is who we are.

SOME FAMILY TRADITIONS I CHERISH ARE:

1. Thanksgiving reunions of our entire extended Florida family on Sanibel Island, accompanied by turkey and all the trimmings.
2. While growing up, suppertime at 6:00 p.m. Everyone knew it; everyone was there. Suppertime was our 'sit-down talk-time.'

MANY PEOPLE ASK: 'When should we change a tradition?'

THE ANSWER: We should change a tradition when it becomes counterproductive.

EXAMPLE: Our 6:00 p.m. dinnertime was special because of *what happened* when we gathered at six, not the exact time. When I became night school principal for the Adult Education program, it was no longer possible to eat at 6:00 p.m. If I wanted to maintain our family sit-down talk-time I had to change the time. It was changed to 4:00 p.m. to maintain and preserve the special time together. IT WORKED!

POINTERS FOR PARENTS

1. IDENTIFY YOUR FAMILY TRADITIONS. Communicate these to the children and the reason for their importance.
2. SHARE THE HISTORY OF THE TRADITION: How long has it been in your family? Why is it important to your family?

REMEMBER: Your traditions carry values and identity. Maintain them as long as they deliver the values and priorities of your family.

♦ TEAMWORK ♦

Teamwork isn't just for the playing field. Teamwork is important in the family. Once parents realize the difficulty and complexity of parenthood, they'll agree teamwork is needed between Mom and Dad. Once both parents agree to work as a team, parenting becomes more fun and meaningful. Each parent's strengths should be realized and put to work for the benefit of the entire family. The first step is for both parents to admit that one parent *cannot* do it alone. Both parents working together create a positive, cooperative, loving atmosphere for the children.

To have teamwork we need a team. This is when it is an advantage to have two parents with the children. When there is a divorce, it not only tears kids apart from the inside out, it breaks up the entire team. The team spirit disappears. When a family splits up, it takes extensive rebuilding efforts to get the family to function as a team again.

Look at your own home team to see who the members are. Is there a leader? Is there a captain? Does everyone know their role within the team? Are there certain responsibilities that each team player has, with the knowledge and skills to carry them out?

As the parents, or the co-captains, of this team it is our job to communicate each family member's role. We need to communicate the expectations of each team player.

The parents, or leaders, set the tone and the example. In order to expect the players to act as a team, the parents as leaders, need to demonstrate team spirit. We can't expect the children to cooperate if the parents do not.

The parents should examine their role within the family. In our family, my husband was the sports-minded one who instilled the value of sports teamwork within our daughter. Sports became the springboard of many values he passed on: hope, endurance, teamwork, winning, losing and 'when exhausted, reach for that one last ounce of energy and use it!' It must have made a lasting impression on our daughter because she still talks about it today. As an adult, she often needs to retrieve that 'one last ounce of energy' after a hard day at the office to continue her workday at home.

When we are immersed in those busy parenting years, we may not even realize the impact we are making on our children until they are adults. The son or daughter may recall the parental teaching moment while in their adult lives. It is that instant when we say: "Gee, I didn't know that had such an impact on you."

While my husband may have instilled the values associated with sports, I proudly claim the credit for instilling the value of a good sale. Or, more aptly put: the value of the dollar, especially when it is earned. While our daughter was a teenager we had our usual heated discussions at the mall regarding the benefits of buying items on sale. It seemed she always wanted those name-brand items. I know, some things never change. It was a matter of years before we could say a shopping trip was, once again, enjoyable. I never realized the impact those discussions had on her until she was twenty-two and insisted we go to a consignment shop to purchase jeans, because as she said: "There's no sense in paying those high dollar prices for denim." I don't think she ever noticed the sparkle or tear in my eye as I simply smiled and exclaimed: "All right!"

The point of the story: By practicing teamwork, my husband and I each contributed important values within the family.

POINTERS FOR PARENTS

1. THINK about your and your spouse's strengths. Ask how you can share this huge responsibility of parenting. It was not meant to be done alone.
2. DISCUSS AND DECIDE how you two might share this responsibility. What can each of you contribute? Rely on each parent's talents.
3. Be sure to tell the children the IMPORTANT ROLE each parent has.

REMEMBER: We want to be a part of a winning family team! Each parent has special gifts and talents to pass along to the children. Take time out from your busy day to realize the special gifts you can give your child.

Dr. Carol Kennedy

♦ TABLE TALK ♦

While growing up with four siblings and two parents, a favorite time for all was dinnertime. It was the same time every evening: 6:00 p.m. It was so special the phone was taken off the hook so we would not be disturbed. My father would enter the house at 5:30 p.m. every day, splash water through his hair and comb it straight back. He'd then sit in the corner chair, glance through the newspaper and half-listen to the drone of the television. Aromas wafted through the house as Mom put the finishing touches on dinner.

"Dinner's ready!" was announced at 5:55 p.m. and, by 6:00 p.m., we were all seated in our designated places. Grace was said and the dinner commenced.

Chatter and pleasantries were exchanged as the numerous dishes were passed. My mom and dad took turns inquiring of each child's day. If you had a good day and good grades the conversation was easy, but if it was a day you really didn't want to share you tried to encourage another to talk. My parents usually picked up on that and would, of course, then zero in on the one reluctant to talk. The entire scene seemed too familiar, too routine, and yet we all looked forward to it.

We all had to say something. We joked, we laughed and sometimes argued. I remember the dinner table being a special place where many memorable moments took place. Some of my most vivid childhood memories centered around that table.

While raising our daughter, my husband and I naturally continued this tradition. However, because we both worked outside the home, there were a few changes. I didn't spend hours preparing a meal, nor was it always at 6:00 p.m. The important ingredient remained: We ate together, at the dinner table. It became our arena for talking, joking, asking and answering.

It wasn't until our daughter's teen years that we began to notice the table talk diminishing. We felt something was missing and when we realized what it was—we took action. You know the saying: 'You don't know what you've got until you lose it.' We evaluated the situation and discovered there were two days during the week which were extremely hectic with after-school activities and meetings. We all decided if we couldn't all eat together on those days, we would at least set aside a time to have a snack and cover daily happenings. The new snack time proved to be equally special. It was in the early evening, and it served the purpose; we were talking and we were together.

Here are some ideas to get your *TABLE TALK started.*

POINTERS FOR PARENTS

1. FOCUS on dinnertime as a priority. Examine schedules to choose appropriate times. Discuss this new time as a new tradition in your family.
2. LOOK at weekly interruptions to this new tradition. Is there a day or two when this is impossible? If so, then improvise and plan a snack time.
3. PLAN a specific dinnertime. Tell everyone to arrive 15 minutes before the time. This gives you a window to allow for the unexpected. This gives you a chance to emphasize: *wash your hands!*
4. CHOOSE a dinner place: at the table, at the kitchen bar?
5. TURN OFF the television. This is your quality family time to converse and enjoy dinner together.

NOTE: If this is a new family tradition, you may encounter resistance and questions. That is normal. Just remind them this is a new way to spend time with each other and talk about the day.

REMEMBER: Table talk can be the center of many memorable moments. Without a doubt, it will become a favorite time of the day. Table talk will create a center of communication.

♦ TALK TO YOUR KIDS! ♦

My neighbor complains: "My kids won't talk to me." A co-worker admits with exasperation:

"I don't know where my daughter is; she never tells me." A single parent, exhausted, confides: "I don't know who my son's hanging around with."

Have you heard these comments before: from a friend, neighbor, or in your own home? I've heard them countless times from friends, neighbors and relatives. When they ask for my opinion, I offer it.

Often, parents prefer the sugar-coated solution rather than the dose of 'reality.' If we don't activate ourselves to be part of the solution, we will be part of the problem, resulting in children who are out of control. It's true that an ounce of prevention is worth a pound of cure.

Good kids quickly find an alternative route to good behavior if the parents aren't monitoring and guiding their actions.

Each of the introductory three statements is a symptom of the same problem: lack of communication and control of the children. If we lose communication or control we lose our kids. THE FIRST STEP IS THIS: If you think you've lost communication with or control of your children, begin today to rectify the situation.

RESPONSE TO THE FIRST STATEMENT: *"My kids won't talk to me."*

Remember, we are the adult parents. It's our job to initiate conversations. Kids are kids and it is not their job to build or strengthen the communication lines. It is ours.

FIRST SCENARIO:

PARENT: "Hi, how was your day?"

KIDS: "Uh, okay."

PARENT: "What do you mean? What happened?"

KIDS: "Nothin'."

PARENT: "I don't believe that for a moment . . . tell me about your morning."

The point is—keep asking. Keep probing. Get specific. Mention a particular time or person to zero in on a topic.

Many parents will give up after the first "uh, okay." Kids quickly learn not to give details if parents don't want them.

RESPONSE TO THE SECOND STATEMENT: *"I don't know where my kids are; they never tell me."*

HOLD IT RIGHT THERE! They'd better tell you. And you'd better expect an answer. Maintain your parental rights and responsibilities. It's a major problem if we don't know where our kids are. If we don't know where they are, we certainly don't know what they are doing either.

Many parents I've counseled never questioned the children when they were growing up. As children approach the teen years, many parents say they are afraid to begin questioning. *Do not be afraid.*

Once you've decided to keep better track of the children, tell everyone in the family. Inform them that you may have been a little lax before, but you are changing and will expect to know and approve of their whereabouts. Apologize to the children for not keeping better track in the past. You'll be amazed at the positive reaction this brings.

SECOND SCENARIO:

PARENT: "Where are you going?"
KIDS: "Out."
PARENT: "Out where?"
KIDS: "Oh, you know, out."
PARENT: "No, I don't know—where?"
KIDS: "You never asked before. Why should I tell you now?"
PARENT: "Because I should have asked before. I made a mistake. From now on, I want to know and approve of where you are going, before you go . . .*This is the new rule of the house."*

The point is: Ask and they will tell you.

When parents don't ask where kids are going, they think we don't care. If we don't ask where they are going, kids are relying on 'kid judgment' and their peers' opinion. I think we know where that can lead.

RESPONSE TO THE THIRD STATEMENT: *"I don't know who my kids are hanging around with now."*

STOP RIGHT THERE! FIND OUT! This is critical and is a must to good parenting. The old adage 'Your friends are your mirrors and show you yourself' is truest during the teen years. If you've lost touch on this one, reassert yourself and find out who your children are socializing with at the present. WHY? IF THE CHILD IS NOT GETTING VALUES AND APPROVAL FROM THE PARENTS, THEY WILL FIND SOMEWHERE ELSE TO GET IT.

THIRD SCENARIO:

PARENT: "Who was that you were walking with in the neighborhood?"

KIDS: "Nobody important."

PARENT: "I didn't say they were important; I want to know *who* they are and *where* they live."

KIDS: "Why? It's none of your business."

PARENTS: "Wrong—it's every bit of my business—I'm responsible for you until you are legally an adult . . .I'm your parent."

The point is: It's not only our business to know what our kids are doing; it's our responsibility.

POINTERS FOR PARENTS

1. Tell the children you will be keeping track of their activities and friends. Remind them that it is your RESPONSIBILITY as their parent. They don't have to like it, and yes, it is true, 'Life is not fair.'
2. Let the children know they need your PERMISSION before they consent to activities with their friends.
3. Expect resistance from them, if this is a new approach for you. COMMUNICATE to the family what to expect from you. *Be assured that you are doing the right thing.*

REMEMBER: We need to know *where* our children are, *what* they are doing and *whom* they are with. Children need and want direction from us, even though they don't admit it.

♦ TV SENSE ♦

The television brings people into our homes we would not otherwise invite. We simply click the remote to receive our guests in all shapes and sizes. Did you ever think about the quality of the person we allow into our homes via the television screen? Consider the amount of time the uninvited guest spends with our children. It is common in households for a large amount of the viewing time to be unsupervised by the parents.

There has been much discussion regarding the impact of TV upon the viewer. Researchers do not agree on the permanence or the negative impact of the television. Of course, there are also excellent, high-quality programs beneficial to our children. I draw the conclusion: If the good television shows have a positive impact on the viewer, why wouldn't the violent shows have a negative effect on the viewer?

As parents, we need to rely on our intelligence and common sense. If we're watching a show that makes us uncomfortable or appears too violent or explicit, we simply turn it off. A television program is just that—a television program.

There are two ways for children to watch the TV: with, or without the parents. If they are watching it alone, they are drawing their own conclusions and choosing their own programs. Depending upon the age of the child, he may not really know if the program is reality or fantasy. If the parents accompany the child during viewing, they can explain and censor as needed.

Children today live in a world far different from our childhood surroundings. They see and hear about children being gunned down in their neighborhoods and schools. We see children killing parents and parents killing children. This can be seen on the *news* and in regularly scheduled programs.

It makes sense to monitor the quality and quantity of TV viewing. Be aware of the violence and sexual content. In addition, be mindful of the commercial content. Ask yourself what the commercials are advertising to your child.

Next, observe the manner in which your children watch the television. If they are sitting within inches or a few feet of the screen, move them back. Take notice of the child's demeanor. If they are so *tuned in* to the TV that everything else is *tuned out*, this is being too involved.

A popular question is: What difference does it make what my children watch? It's only TV. It's not real. The answer to that is: It is only make believe to those children who *know* the difference. It is only make believe to those children who have been taught right from wrong and directed by their parents.

A growing number of children are left alone to determine their own reality. Many children consider the television their window of reality. If the parent is not present to assist in the process, children decide for themselves.

On several occasions, while teaching middle school, I've listened to children argue over what is right and wrong. Often they revert to quoting a sit-com or movie as a source of the truth. When I attempted to explain the difference between fictional shows and reality the response was merely: "Oh, I didn't know that."

POINTERS FOR PARENTS

1. MONITOR television time. Know what and when the children are watching TV.
2. SET HOUSE RULES for acceptable TV viewing. Allow certain times for TV viewing. Communicate to the children what is acceptable and what is off-limits and why.

3. *JUST SAY NO! Have the courage to turn off the television if you feel it is overused.*

4. OFFER ALTERNATIVES: crafts, gardening, games, board games, physical exercise or water games. Parents need to take the initiative—children will not think of this by themselves.

5. ENJOY the good shows TOGETHER! Plan a special snack and set aside time for that favorite show.

REMEMBER: As the parent, take charge of the TV time in your household. Often, the TV brings people into the home we would not otherwise invite. Television content can have a great impact on children. We need to be sure it is a positive one!

♦ THE POWER OF WORDS! ♦

Did you know that the single largest indicator of a person's intelligence is his/her vocabulary? In the business world, promotions have been linked to the level of the individual's vocabulary. Words mean things and words have power. The ability to string words together in an intelligent and meaningful way is admired. The ability to vary one's vocabulary according to the audience is a skill few people possess. The way a person enunciates words carries its own message.

Think about people you know and their command of the English language. Think about the people whom you would deem 'successful' in life. Consider the superintendent, mayor, teacher or minister you most admire. Do they have a strong command of the English language? When someone is in a leadership role and they are not an effective public speaker, do we think less of them?

Consider television personalities who can speak properly and use appropriate vocabulary. The first impression may be that they are intelligent and know their subject. First impressions are lasting ones, and may be the only impression we receive.

There are occasions when the first impression is the wrong impression. That is unfortunate, but it does happen. For example: Often, teenagers choose to use language that is less than intelligent. The adult listener gets the first impression that the young person is not very bright. The conclusion was based on mere minutes of conversation.

This may not be fair, but it is a fact of life. I have been guilty of the very same thing. As a teacher, at the beginning of each school year, I drew quick, first impressions from the 150 students I taught. We have two things visible to us immediately: a person's looks and words. I must admit, most of the time I was right, but occasionally a very bright student would choose to speak in single syllables or mimic a television character.

I would actually confront the student with: "Why are you talking like that? Don't you know it sounds ignorant?" They would then identify the cartoon character they were mimicking and reply: "Oh, I didn't know it made me sound stupid." Sometimes it just takes an adult correcting the child firmly but compassionately to make a great difference.

Children's vocabulary begins to be developed at a very young age—in their infancy. It is important to use the correct word for objects and people when children are young. As parents, we can set the stage for vocabulary growth and development.

Words are the building blocks within our English language. There are many activities we can provide in the home to identify the importance and power of words.

POINTERS FOR PARENTS

1. When children are young, begin to name objects and people. Point to the object and name it: chair, bike, book, etc. Enunciate the word clearly. Look at the child when you say the word. You'll know this has had an impact when you see the child mouthing the words as you say them. When our daughter was six months old, she began to mimic the lip movements. As a young parent, I didn't realize the importance of that at the time. As our daughter grew up, I realized the impact the enunciation had on her vocabulary development. Her vocabulary skills were always above grade level.
2. AVOID baby talk. This will keep the child in the baby talk stage longer than she/he should be.
3. As the child gets older, PLAY as many word games as possible. Play with them to show the importance you place on vocabulary.
4. CHOOSE WORD GAMES that are challenging, fun and age appropriate.
5. WALK AND TALK: When children are young, take them for walks and talk about what you see. Identify objects as you walk.

REMEMBER: If words are the building blocks of our language, we can help build a strong foundation. Consider the age of the child when you focus on your vocabulary activities.

♦DO YOU KNOW WHERE YOUR KIDS ARE?♦

Whether I am serving on a Juvenile Justice committee or reading the daily newspaper about the most recent horrific killing by kids, the same haunting questions pop into my mind:

Where were the parents? Didn't they know what their kids were doing? How could parents not know there were guns in the teen's bedroom?

When parents fail to parent, the worst-case scenario is that children will end up with no knowledge of right and wrong and, consequently, make their own rules of life, committing a serious crime. The least-case scenario is that the teens will be just a little wild and rebellious but once adulthood is reached, will acknowledge mistakes and be fine: just a phase, so to speak.

That is a gamble I would not want to take. The gamble parents take while barely supervising the children is that the least-case scenario will be played out rather than the worst-case scenario. There are no guarantees when the parent surrenders control of the children and has no knowledge of the children's whereabouts. Today, there are far too many scenarios like that one reported on the front page.

Personally, I would rather be the parent who disciplines, directs and knows where my children are.

I have discovered, over the past several years, that there are too many parents who really do not know where their children are, and have no intention of finding out. This has always shocked me because my husband and I were a parenting team that shared the duties, knew our daughter's friends and discussed her activities.

Granted, especially during the teen years, parents witness rebellion and peer pressure and children may not always tell us the whole truth. Looking back to my teen years, I admit there were a few times I did not tell my parents the whole truth. However, they always knew whom they could call if I wasn't home by curfew. Likewise, my husband and I knew our daughter's friends and whom to call, should we suspect or wonder about her location.

NOTE: Parents need to know their children's friends and activities. It is normal and a part of growing up to withhold some details from parents.

ASK YOURSELF: Do I know where my kids are? If you do not, find out. And after you find out, ask yourself: Do I approve? Is this okay?

Parents have the right and the responsibility to monitor and control the activities of their children.

The following comment is unacceptable from any child: "It's none of your business." It is the parents' business and should be a number-one priority in the household.

EXAMPLE: During recent years my husband and I have heard on numerous occasions, whether at school or in our neighborhoods: 'I don't have any idea where our son/daughter is; they never tell us.'

RED FLAG! Do you think there is a problem with that parent/child relationship? Should children have total autonomy and privileges to do whatever they want, whenever they want?

The answer is NO! Parenting is to be done by the parents, not the children. If it were a child's job, it would be called 'childrening.' And 'childrening' would be about as ridiculous as the sound of the newly formed word.

You may be asking yourself: What can I do? I realize I have been too lenient with my children, and have not provided the necessary guidance. Now, they are in their teens and I have no control.

ANSWER: Parents need to decide and agree upon a change of approach with the children before implementing it in the household. Proceed in the direction of reclaiming control.

POINTERS FOR PARENTS

1. First: Parents should EVALUATE current parenting practices and decide if improvement is needed after they've answered the question: Do we know where our kids are? Do we know the names of their friends? No exceptions, no excuses.
2. If you've lost CONTROL of the children, you need to get it back.
3. TELL all members of the family about your new parenting approach.
4. The children will resist at first, but in the long run children know parents care when they provide RULES AND INVOLVEMENT.
5. FIND OUT the names, addresses and phone numbers of best friends and acquaintances.
6. LOOK IN THEIR ROOMS. The bedroom is the signature of your child's values and priorities. Examine the posters and music.

REMEMBER: If you're a parent, everything the children do is your business. And it is also your responsibility. When someone asks you, "Do you know where your kids are?" you want to be able to shout YES!

♦ XYZ ... CONCLUSION ♦

I hope you have found the wide range of parenting tips, from A to Z, informative and useful. Accompanying this job of parenting are the givens: Parenting is a comprehensive job, full of responsibilities, rewards, emotions, and stages of development. It is comforting to know we are not alone in this job we call parenting.

All parents will have their good days and their bad days. I hope this book will have the effect of increasing the number of good days. It is important that we do the very best we can and conduct our parenting in an atmosphere of love and care.

If we remember that discipline is a gift, wrapped in love and kindness, our parenting will include all the necessary ingredients of teaching, guiding and nurturing.

As you begin to incorporate the Pointers for Parents into your parenting, you will notice an added sense of security and joy. The smart parent is the one who realizes help is needed, seeks it out, and implements the suggestions.

Good luck and happy parenting!

Dr. Carol Kennedy

Part Two

Literacy: Cracking the Code

◆◆◆◆◆◆◆◆◆◆◆

Introduction

Part two is devoted entirely to the subject of literacy and the parents' role in preparation and enhancement of it. Numerous aspects of reading and the lasting impact of parents' involvement complement one another.

The phrase 'crack the code' refers to the process beginning readers experience as they are taught methods to give meaning to the printed word. A code may be as simple as the pronunciation of a letter's sound or as complex as attacking a twenty-letter word. The 'Crack the Code' series is comprised of fifteen separate articles, each addressing a unique reading skill. Practical pointers for parents are always included for easy implementation.

♦ READING IS A FAMILY AFFAIR ♦ -SOME BASICS-

As parents, one of the most important things we can do is prepare the children for reading success. The parent is the child's first teacher and the home is the child's first school.

What parents say and do in the home is repeated by the children.

Not many will argue with the notion that reading is essential to success in and out of school. Reading is needed in all subjects in school and all careers chosen, in differing degrees.

As a parent and reading specialist, I can confirm the importance of reading in and out of school. *Reading is a process in which the written symbol is transformed into contextual meaning.* Reading is to the mind what physical exercise is to the body.

Parents do not have to be reading specialists to lay the foundation for reading. The first five years are the most important in forming a child's values and basic characteristics. Research is clear on this subject: Children who are ready to learn when they enter school do learn in school. While my daughter was a preschooler, I incorporated the following pointers into our home. She was reading by the time she was four years old, and to this day, maintains her exceptional reading speed and comprehension. She loves to read!

NOTE: The parent is the child's first teacher. If you can incorporate the following tips into your home, your children may be on their way to reading success.

POINTERS FOR PARENTS

1. **Hold** your children and read aloud to them. You can begin this when they are infants. The melodic sound of your voice and the book's presence begin to make a positive impression.

2. **Note** your child's crawling: I have discovered through my experiences as a reading specialist that many children who never crawl have difficulty reading. Knowledge and coordination of the left to right movement are essential. In remedial reading situations I have had to get on the floor with children and teach them how to crawl. The crawling actually readies the brain for the left-to-right movement needed in the successful reading process. If the concept of left and right is not firmly planted, the reader's eyes may travel all over the page.

3. **Reinforce** left and right. Determine the child's knowledge by saying: "Raise your right hand . . . Raise your left hand . . . lift your right foot, left foot." While in a car, point out objects: "Look to the right and see the cows . . . Look to the left and see the garbage truck." Statements such as these are a good diagnosis point.

4. **Create** activities of your own: Using your child's interests and hobbies, create activities revolving around them. For example: While riding their bike, "Turn left at the next corner . . . Look at the blue house on the right . . . Hang that poster on the wall to your left." The possibilities are endless.

REMEMBER: Because reading is a left-to-right skill, it is essential that children know the difference. As parents are the children's first teacher, what is done in the first five years can make the difference between success and failure in and out of school.

♦ PARENTS ARE TEACHERS TOO! ♦

ATTENTION PARENTS! Whether we like the idea or not—we are our children's first teachers. As the parents, we see our children the most during the first five years. The direction we give. . . the values we instill, last a lifetime. One of the most important skills we can begin to instill in our children is the skill of reading. Don't panic! I'm not issuing all parents certificates to perform as reading specialists. I'm going to give you some helpful hints that will give your child an edge or head start in the reading process. Yes, it is a *process.* Good reading skills take many years to develop, and the process continues into adulthood.

As a matter of fact, what we *do* as parents during the first five years is extremely difficult to *'undo.'* We can use that fact to our advantage and do everything we can to create effective readers in our household. We can never be accused of helping our children *too* much with reading.

Like most parents, my husband and I did the best we knew how to do in the parenting department. We incorporated the following reading tips and our daughter began reading at the age of four. That superior reading skill carried through into her adult life. She was able to complete her homework faster and maintain good grades. She is an avid reader today. Because she mastered the basics of reading early, she was able to concentrate on her comprehension and speed.

Once we know the types of skills our children need, our imagination and common sense can take over. Here are some suggestions to get you started with your children.

POINTERS FOR PARENTS

1. Emphasize the left-to-right movement: A reader's eyes travel from left to right. While reading aloud to the children, move your finger from left to right to show the left-to-right movement. If children do not know the difference between right and left, the reading process will be confusing to them. As parents we can directly teach children "This is the right hand, this is the left." Raise your right hand with them. Hint: turn your back to them as you raise the right and left. If you face them, it becomes more confusing. Practice right and left with the hands and feet. Get on the floor and move around as much as you wish. Play games which incorporate right and left such as: Bingo, Twister floor game, Hokey-Pokey circle game. Incorporate left and right questions while riding the bikes or traveling in the car: " Look at the red truck on the right hand side . . ." The more you practice right and left, the better they will become at this. You want 'left and right' to become second nature to the children.

2. Ask yourself: Did your children ever crawl? Experience and research have shown that if children do not crawl, they may lack the knowledge and 'feel' of the left and the right side of the body. If the child did not crawl, you may need to practice more left and right movement. Or, I have seen parents and teachers get down on the floor and crawl with the children. This has been known to be highly effective.

3. Read aloud and read together: As parents, we set the tone in our household. As parents, we set the pace. We also set the examples our children will follow. If we tell them we think reading is important, they will think positively about reading.

If we make a point to read for enjoyment every day, they will get the message that "Mom and Dad even read, and they think it's fun." They may not verbalize it to us, but they are getting that impression. The saying: Your actions speak so loud I can't hear what you say, is alive and well here. Talk about reading. Talk about your favorite book or author. If you don't have a favorite author, find one, and tell them why you like that author.

REMEMBER: Whether we like the notion or not, we are our children's first teachers. We can put our children on the road to reading success. Our children will be grateful and will thank us for it later. Good luck and good reading!

♦ INTRODUCTION ♦ CRACK THE CODE SERIES

If you are reading this you have learned to "crack the code." This refers to cracking the phonetic code of the English language. Cracking the Code is better known as phonics and word-attack skills in the world of reading.

To crack the code of English is to learn the twenty-six letters of the alphabet, master their sounds, then transform the printed symbol into meaning. Once this is accomplished, we can decode and begin to experience the joy of reading.

The best time to prepare children for literacy is during the preschool years. Once prepared, children will be eager and ready to learn as they enter school.

My conversations with parents regarding the importance of reading usually did not change: "If they don't get the basics by third grade, they won't get it. They will be playing catch-up for the remainder of their school years."

YOU MAY BE THINKING: *Oh no, I can't prepare my kids for reading: I'm not a reading teacher! As a matter of fact, I never even went to college.*

MY RESPONSE IS: "Oh yes, you can!" As soon as parents know what to do, it can be easy and enjoyable. My experience with parent consultations has shown that parents welcome practical tips to help their children succeed in reading. Parents are grateful and excited about incorporating the practical tips into the home activities.

I continue to have great faith and high expectations in parents' desire and ability to raise children. Once parents have the knowledge, they gladly share it with their children.

Parents: Always consider the child's age and size as you apply the suggestions.

The next fifteen articles address a unique aspect of 'cracking the code.'

CRACK THE CODE - #1
Questions for the School

Parents often forget that the schools may be their greatest resource for information regarding their children's reading successes or failures. Don't be shy when it comes to asking questions about your children's skills. Remember: the only dumb question is the one that is never asked.

Often, parents show frustration and concern about the literacy level of their children. Parents question the school's policy of 'phonics avoidance.' Parents wonder why their middle-school child cannot pronounce words that a third grader should know. Or, they ask how their child can be receiving A's and B's in reading and English and be in remedial reading class. That's a good question.

As parents, we have the right and responsibility to find out about the school's reading program. Research and experience have taught me that it is imperative a child have a solid phonics and word-attack foundation by the **end of the third grade.**

In my 28 years as a reading specialist and school administrator, I always tell parents regarding reading skills:

"If they don't have it by the third grade, they won't get it . . . The child will be playing catch-up the rest of their school years."

There are a few basic questions you can ask your school staff for some initial information.

POINTERS FOR PARENTS
Questions to Ask the School Regarding Your Child's Reading

1. **First,** find out about the school's reading program. Ask: What reading program does the school use? What reading

series is used in the elementary and middle schools? Get the name of the publisher and reading series.

2. **Second,** find out about the organization of the reading program. Ask: What role does phonics play in the reading process? In what grades is phonics stressed? Phonics should play a major role in the early elementary years. I have had some school staff members reply that they do not teach phonics. If they do not teach phonics, the kids will not learn it and that's an invitation to trouble in the reading department.

3. **Third,** what reading skills should my child know by January? By June? Ask for a list of the reading skills with examples. Each teacher should have a reading curriculum for each grade level.

TIP: Reading programs should have a balance of phonics, sight words, vocabulary study and comprehension. Teachers in the early grades need to emphasize the skills to crack the code: phonics.

The hierarchy of skills can appear complex, but much of it is common sense. Certain skills must be mastered before others can be attempted.

REMEMBER: If you can read this, you have learned to crack the code. Be sure your child has also learned the code of phonics.

CRACK THE CODE - #2
The Basics

You may notice that the following five pointers for parents will be repeated throughout the 'Crack the Code' series. For literacy and language development, the pointers continually emerge as necessary for a solid foundation.

In the English alphabet there are 26 letters. Of the 26 letters, 16 make only one sound and ten make more than one sound. How's that for a quick review of the beginnings of what we learned if we learned phonics: the tools to begin to crack the code.

I'm going to take a huge risk here and claim that it is the primary responsibility of the schools to teach reading in the elementary grades; but, it is the parents' responsibility to prepare the children for reading and provide practice time during 'homework.' Children who enter school ready to learn, will learn.

POINTERS FOR PARENTS

Parents: Always consider the child's age and size as you incorporate your common sense into the suggestions

1. **From infancy through childhood,** hold the child on your lap and read. Read enjoyable books to the child with enthusiasm and expression. Let them know reading is fun for you, the parent.
2. **During Infancy**: When you speak to the child look at him/her and enunciate your words. Let the child see your lips and often the child will want to touch your lips. This is a positive sign of interest and understanding of sounds.

3. **Walk and Talk:** As you and your child are walking around the house or outdoors, walk and talk at the same time. Talk about what you see and name the objects. Soon, the child will begin to repeat the words. Again, let the child see your mouth and the way you are making the sounds. Can you see how this is leading to the pronunciation of the words?

4. **Left and Right:** Because reading is a left-to-right skill, it is essential that the child know the difference between right and left. If the child is confused about left and right, his eyes will travel all over the page. Left and right knowledge can begin when your child begins to crawl. Think about it: left to right knowledge, muscle and nerve coordination are needed for the crawling. It is important that your child learns to crawl. During my private tutoring sessions, it has been necessary to determine if the child ever learned to crawl. If not, it may be incorporated into the session. When I ask the parents, they often surprise themselves when they respond: 'Well, no, she/he went right into walking!'

5. **Follow the finger** from left to right as you read aloud to children. Finger reading is acceptable for very early readers as it helps train the eyes for the left-to-right movement. However, the finger reading should be eliminated by the fourth grade.

REMEMBER: By incorporating the pointers into your parenting you are helping children crack the code. Once children crack the code, they decode and begin to apply meaning to sounds on the page. Then they're on their way to reading enjoyment and success.

CRACK THE CODE - #3
Oral Reading Activities

When reading aloud, both parents and children should participate. Oral reading activities set the stage for more reinforcement of left and right eye movement, and proper pronunciation and inflection.

POINTERS FOR PARENTS

1. **Right and Left:** Determine if your child knows the difference between right and left. Say to her/him: 'raise your right hand . . .raise your left hand' While traveling: 'Look at that ice cream truck to the left . . . Look at that new store going up on the right . . .Look at that new bike Jimmy is riding, to your right.' The point is to incorporate the 'right and left' direction into many conversations. This will reveal the child's knowledge of right and left. You will then know how to proceed.

FOR EXAMPLE: If you determine your child is weak in the left and right knowledge, incorporate activities into the day. Personally, I like the Twister and Hokey-Pokey game. The Twister Game is a floor mat with various colored circles. Cards drawn will say: 'Put your right hand on the red spot, left hand on the green, right foot on the purple and left foot on the yellow.' It's great fun as children giggle when they become entangled with their friends. It's fun for any age and is a great learning tool.

HOKEY-POKEY: This is the song frequently played at wedding receptions. Everyone gets in a circle, holds hands and listens to commands such as: 'put your right foot in, put your right foot out, put your right foot in and shake it all about. Do the hokey pokey as you turn yourself around. That's what it's all about!' I've seen people of all ages have fun with this.

2. **READ-ALOUD-TIME:** Parents initiate reading aloud. If you have a child who loves to read and is a good reader, this is a natural. Children are usually reluctant if they are not good readers. It can be embarrassing and humiliating to them, especially if older siblings make fun of them.

GUIDELINES:

a. Help children choose an appropriate book. Find one that is enjoyable and fairly easy to read.

b. Set the example of reading aloud with verbal and facial expressions.

c. Ask for volunteers to read. If they do not volunteer, begin to ask questions: 'Why don't you want to read aloud?' 'Would you like to try it next time?'

If children continually refuse to read aloud, there is probably a good reason. If you don't get an answer from the child, call the school and ask the child's reading level. Ask the teacher for book suggestions. Or, ask the librarian for assistance.

It's important to ensure the child is choosing a book that is not too difficult for reading aloud. We want to produce reading success, especially when reading aloud. Reading success builds confidence.

REMEMBER: Stress the knowledge of right and left with exciting oral reading, and you'll help your child 'crack the code.'

CRACK THE CODE - #4
Categorizing

An essential reading skill is categorizing. When we categorize we put things in an order or groups. Categorizing is the beginning of organizing. It sets a solid foundation for the thinking process, necessary for more advanced reading skills. Categorizing can take various shapes and forms.

Are you already thinking of different ways to organize or put household items in categories?

For example: think about the dishwasher, silverware organizer, drawers, the bedrooms, garage, laundry room or the yard. Do they need any organization?

Let's begin with simple objects before moving to the bedroom or garage.

POINTERS FOR PARENTS

1. **Silverware Drawer:** How do you organize the silverware? We have a silverware holder which clearly shows places for the different utensils. Take the utensils and say:

   'This is the place for the knives to go; this is where the spoons go.'

   I remember when my daughter was three, she loved to put the silverware away in all the right places. She still loved it when she was four and five. As she grew up she lost interest in that activity and we would think of others.

2. **The dishwasher:** The dishwasher has places for silverware, cups, glasses, plates and larger items. Explain to the children what goes where and why.

3. **The drawers:** They are everywhere! Choose a drawer that can be completed fairly quickly. Then the child will make progress and want to do more.

Ask the children for suggestions: Should we organize the drawer by color, items, or by size?

REMEMBER: Even though these tasks are regular chores to us, they can be valuable learning tools for children. Give the activities a try and enjoy this creative time with your child.

CRACK THE CODE - #5
Attacking Word Parts

To successfully crack the code for large words, readers need to know how to decipher small parts of the word. This reading skill is known as word attack. One method is to attack the prefix. A prefix is a small word part added to the beginning of a base word. The prefix changes the meaning of the word.

To learn prefixes, the child will need to be at or above the third-grade level of reading. Prefix knowledge helps to unlock the meaning of words. A prefix is a small word part added to the beginning of a base or root word.

FOR EXAMPLE: When you see a word you do not know, how do you begin to pronounce or 'attack' the word?

One method of 'attack' is to look for small word parts, pronounce them and derive the meaning. This makes the decoding process manageable, bringing success to the reader.

The best way to describe prefixes is through an example:

PREFIX	ROOT WORD	WHOLE WORD	MEANING
un	happy	unhappy	not happy
dis	belief	disbelief	no belief
pre	game	pregame	before game
post	game	postgame	after game

Notice how the tiny prefix changed the entire meaning of the word. Prefixes and root words are everywhere. They are in the newspapers, magazines, billboards, radio and television.

The key is to know the meanings of those prefixes. If we know the meaning of the prefix, we are on our way to knowing the whole word.

POINTERS FOR PARENTS

1. Your child is ready for **prefix instruction** if they are at the third-grade reading level or above.
2. **Look around the house for prefixes**. The best example may be the sports arena: Announcers and sports writers always mention pre- and post-game activities.
3. **Emphasize** that small parts of a large word can have their own meaning.
4. **Create a chart**: fold a paper so there are 4 columns:

PREFIX	ROOT WORD	WHOLE WORD	MEANING
UN	HAPPY	UNHAPPY	NOT HAPPY

Once children grasp the prefix skill, they enjoy taking the words apart and putting them back together.

REMEMBER: The decoding skill of prefixes is a necessity for the child's reading 'tool kit.' Once you discover all the places prefixes hide, you'll wonder why you didn't notice them sooner. Have fun with prefixes.

CRACK THE CODE - #6
Syllable City

Another way to decipher small parts of a word is through syllable attack. If the reader can unlock the meaning of each syllable in a word, then the meaning of the whole word is clear.

DEFINITION OF SYLLABLE: A small 'piece' of a word identified by a vowel sound. Every syllable has a vowel sound and every vowel sound has a syllable.

EXAMPLE: cup—one piece, one syllable, one vowel sound
ba-con: two pieces, two syllables, two vowel sounds

WHY ARE SYLLABLES IMPORTANT?
If children can crack the code of the pieces of words, they can pronounce the whole word. Once they can pronounce a word they begin to unlock its meaning.

WHAT IF we aren't sure how many syllables are in a word? Try looking it up in a dictionary. The dictionary entry will show the breaks or pieces of words within the whole word. The pieces of the word will be separated by a hyphen or dot.

POINTERS FOR PARENTS

1. Begin with one-syllable words: dog, bat, down. Say the word aloud. Hit a surface every time you hear a break or piece of the word. You will hit the surface for every vowel sound.

EXAMPLE: bat: one hit, one piece, one syllable; dog: one hit, one piece, one syllable.

2. When the child is sure of one-syllable words, move to two-syllable words.
EXAMPLE: Bacon: ba-con: two hits, two pieces, two syllables; into: in-to: two hits, two pieces, two syllables.

3. Progress to three-syllable words when the child is 100% confident of the one-and two-syllable words.
EXAMPLE: multitude: mul-ti-tude: three hits, three pieces, three syllables.

4. The key to success is 'do not rush.' Once you enter the three-syllable word arena, you are into difficult words. Practice the one- and two-syllable words repeatedly.

5. Once you feel the child knows one and two syllables with 100% accuracy, have them pretend to be the teacher. The parent will role play someone who does not know syllables. It is the child's job to teach the parent, and to be sure the learner understands. Children love this because now, they're in the driver's seat!

6. Think of all the different objects to tap the surface. This, in itself, can be fun for the child: Use pens, pencils, hands or fingers. Be imaginative!

7. Tunes and songs can be created with the syllable hits. One of my favorite commercials is the 'Chili's "I love my baby back, baby back, baby back ribs." The actors hit the table on every syllable.

REMEMBER: Syllable knowledge is a handy tool to help children 'crack the code.' Once children can 'decode,' or read pieces of words, they are ready to tackle or read the whole word.

CRACK THE CODE - #7
Phonics Fun

Many secrets to cracking the code of our language are taught under the heading of 'phonics.' One of the most essential phonics lessons involves vowel sounds. People who are good readers have a sound knowledge of vowel sounds and rules that accompany them. Children who have difficulty with vowel sounds will have difficulty reading because they will not have the 'secrets' to crack the code.

There are usually exceptions to every rule; however, the children and adults I tutor in reading often exhibit a weakness in vowel sounds. Vowel-sound knowledge is the golden key to unlock words, or crack the code.

On the first-grade reading assessment of a local school district, it is clear that short and long vowel sounds are expected in first grade. Short vowels are: hat, bed, hit, hot and hut. Long vowels say their own name: lake, feet, kite, home and cute.

There are many ways to practice vowels at home. My favorite one is to sing the "Old MacDonald Had a Farm" song.

POINTERS FOR PARENTS

Sing the names of the five vowels in order, in the song "Old MacDonald Had a Farm." When you reach the animal sound, use the short sound of each vowel. Then proceed to the long vowel sounds.

EXAMPLE:

Old MacDonald had a farm,
a-e-i-o-u
And on his farm he had some letters,

a-e-i-o-u
With an a, a here and an a, a there,
Here an a, there an a,
Everywhere an a, a
Old MacDonald had a farm,
a-e-i-o-u

Continue through four more verses using a different vowel sound each time.

Recite the short vowel sounds first, then proceed to the long vowel sounds.

The symbol, (like a little smile) above the letter indicates a short vowel. The - symbol above the vowel indicates a long vowel. Remember a long vowel says its name: a - name, e - feet.

Children will have a great time with this song. Adults will, too!

REMEMBER: Old MacDonald Had a Farm A-E-I-O-U! Have fun with this game as you help crack the code. Can you or the children think of other songs in which to insert the vowel sounds?

CRACK THE CODE - #8
Beach Ball Bounce

The game, Beach Ball Bounce, provides practice for two reading skills: letter and sound identification, and differentiation of the left and right. Knowledge of left to right eye movement in reading is so essential it requires frequent monitoring and practice. Letter and sound identification can be applied to consonants and vowels.

POINTERS FOR PARENTS

BEACH BALL BOUNCE

1. Purchase a plastic beach ball that is divided into different colored sections. On each section, print a consonant or vowel with a black permanent marker. If you choose vowels, make them all vowels. If you choose consonants, make them all consonants. It is best to have two beach balls: one for vowels and one for consonants.
2. Take turns bouncing the beach ball to one another. The person who catches the ball recites one word that begins with the letter his/her right thumb is on and one word that begins with the letter his/her left thumb is touching.
3. Notice how you can emphasize the right and left thumb placement to practice knowledge of the right and left. For a younger child, you could also emphasize the colors of the beach ball.

REMEMBER: By playing 'Beach Ball Bounce' at home you can help your children to crack the code of the English language and have fun at the same time. This game can be an enjoyable family activity. Enjoy!

CRACK THE CODE - #9
Junk Mail Search

Unwanted junk mail can serve as a valuable tool to reinforce various reading skills. The family junk mail search is limited only by one's imagination. Adjust the level of difficulty of this activity to include all family members.

If the activity seems too easy, then treat it as a game and explain it is just for fun. If there are younger siblings, explain the importance of the older siblings' involvement to help the younger children. Then they can 'boss' them under the parents' guidance. Children love this!

POINTERS FOR PARENTS

'JUNK-MAIL SEARCH'

1. Collect all the junk mail for a period of time: a week or two weeks. If your junk mail is in short supply, approach the neighbors and ask them to save it for you and the reading project. Or, use magazines and newspapers.
2. Choose a particular set of 'phonics elements' to find in the junk mail.

   For example: vowels: a, e, i, o, u
   blends: bl, gl, fr, or, gr

3. Let the children choose their favorite colored marker.
4. Circle or underline all the words that begin with the letters you choose. Or, cut out the word and paste it on a piece of paper to create a collage.

5. Help each other pronounce the words that are cut out. Discuss the meanings of the words.
6. Be creative: Create stories or songs with the words!

REMEMBER: Activities such as the 'Junk-Mail Search' can help children crack the code. If children experience such enjoyable activities with the entire family they get the message that parents care about reading. Once parents show these skills are important, children attach more value to them. ENJOY!

CRACK THE CODE - #10
Grocery Grab

The activity Grocery Grab can be applied to numerous skill areas. Directions which follow zero in on vowel recognition. Adults and children of all ages love this one!

POINTERS FOR PARENTS

'GROCERY GRAB' FOR VOWELS

1. Materials Needed: Five large paper shopping bags, thick magic markers to label the bags, a variety of empty containers such as boxes, cartons or cans.

2. Explain the difference between long and short vowel sounds: short a, as in hat; short e, as in bet; short i, as in bit; short o, as in hot; and short u, as in hut. Long vowels say their name. Example: long a-cape; long e-heel; long i-bite; long -o boat; long u-cute.

3. Print a large vowel on each bag: A, E, I, O, U

4. Tell the children if you want long or short vowel sounds. As they improve, they can choose either vowel sound. HINT: short vowels are usually more difficult, and should be mastered first.

5. The children will sort the food containers and place them into the appropriate grocery bag. Parents decide: children can toss them or place them.

6. They must say the word aloud, and tell you where the short or long vowel sound is located in the word.

SUGGESTED FOODS:
SHORT VOWELS:

Apples, jam, eggs, ham, chips, popsicles, olives, butter, gum, muffins, cabbage and apple butter.

LONG VOWELS:

Potatoes, cake, raisins, peaches, peas, beans, beets, seeds, cheese, pineapple, rice and yogurt.

You can probably think of many more! Check your cupboards and pantries for more food items to use.

REMEMBER: Games such as Grocery Grab are reinforcing phonics and word-attack skills that will help your children crack the code of the English language. This game can be fun for the whole family and, in the process, the children will become better readers.

CRACK THE CODE - #11
Taxi-Time

Taxi-Time is an activity to reinforce phonics and word-attack skills. You may need to modify the activity to best meet the needs of your family. Due to differing skill levels of family members, encourage older siblings to help younger siblings. All ages have been known to enjoy Taxi-Time.

POINTERS FOR PARENTS

'TAXI-TIME'

In Taxi-Time you are going to build a small village of letters with the help and creativity of the children. There are several streets in the village.

1. Tall Street: consists of all the letters that extend above the line, such as: b, d, f, h, k, l and t
2. Low Street: consists of all the letters that extend below the line, such as: j, p, q, y, and g
3. Friend Street: consists of all the letters that go together to make one sound, such as: ch, sh, th, ng, and wh
4. Vowel Street: consists of all the vowels: a, e, i, o, u
5. Main Street: consists of all the other letters
6. Need more streets? Use your imaginations!

THE GAME: One child is the taxi driver. The rest of the players are passengers. The passengers ask the driver to take them to 'the street where the *girl* lives.' Because 'girl' starts with 'g' and 'g' resides on Low Street, the driver must take them there. If the driver makes a mistake, she/he forfeits the driving privilege and the passenger who recited the word becomes the driver.

Be creative about the other specifics of the game to fit it into your particular situation.

REMEMBER: Games such as Taxi-Time are reinforcing phonics and word-attack skills that will help your children crack the code of the English language. This game can be fun for the whole family and, in the process, the children will become better readers.

CRACK THE CODE - #12
Keyboard Click

Keyboard Click can be applied to beginning or advanced reading skills. It is useful for letter sounds and for more advanced skill levels incorporating vocabulary improvement. Clicks and sounds are needed in this game, allowing the children to make some noise!

POINTERS FOR PARENTS

'KEYBOARD CLICK'

In "Keyboard Click" the parent chooses the area of practice: It could be consonants, vowels, blends or words. If you are not sure which is appropriate, ask the child's teacher. If your child is of preschool age, begin with the letters of the alphabet.

MATERIALS NEEDED:

1. Flash cards: 4"x6" are best.
2. A chair for each participant, facing the caller: The caller can be a parent or child.

SETUP:

1. On each card print, in large letters, the vowel (a, e, i, o, u. and sometimes y); consonant or blend to be included in the game.
2. Each participant gets a chair, which faces the caller: The caller recites the words which have been chosen for the game.

3. Each participant holds a card. The card faces the caller or group in attendance (if this is a classroom or larger group of people).

THE GAME:

The row of players holding the card is the 'keyboard.' Tell the players they are to listen for the beginning, middle or ending sound of the letter they hold. You decide which one. When the child hears the word that contains their sound, she/he should stand up. When she/he stands up she/he can make a clicking sound, like a keyboard makes.

Can you see how children will love making these noises? Their imagination automatically "clicks in" for this game.

For older children, you could incorporate such skills as prefixes (re, non, dis, pre or post) or suffixes: ment, ing, ly, ness and so on.

IMPORTANT WORDS: Another excellent source of 'words to know' is the Dolch word list. The Dolch list is prepared by grade and is a wonderful guide for parents and teachers. Examine the Dolch word list to determine which basic words your child should know. If your child is in third grade, she/he should know all of the words up to their grade. If it is near the end of the school year, the child should know the words on the third grade list, also. The lists or cards can be purchased in a teacher supply store in your area.

REMEMBER: Games such as "Keyboard Click" reinforce phonics and word-attack skills that will help children crack the code of the English language. This game can be fun for the whole family as the children become better readers.

CRACK THE CODE - #13
Ring-A-Letter

Ring-A-Letter encourages all family members to be involved with its construction. Be aware of the children's skill level to individualize the activity as much as possible. Your child's school can provide guidelines for appropriate readings skills.

POINTERS FOR PARENTS

'RING-A-LETTER'

In "Ring-A-Letter" the parent chooses the area of practice: It could be consonants, vowels, blends or words. If you are not sure which is appropriate, ask the teacher. If your child is of preschool age, begin with the letters of the alphabet.

MATERIALS NEEDED:

1. Piece of Styrofoam four inches thick, 30"x20"
2. Nine large primary pencils (or regular pencils)
3. Flash cards
4. Plastic rings. Purchase or cut from plastic lids.

SETUP:

1. Push the nine pencils into the Styrofoam in three equally spaced rows. Write the letters or words on the flash cards. Next to each pencil attach the flash cards to the Styrofoam.

THE GAME:

From a distance of four to eight feet, players try to ring the pencils with the plastic rings. When she/he rings the word, she/he pronounces the letter or word. If they get it right, they score five points. If used appropriately in a sentence, they get another five points.

For older children, you can create additions to the game such as: give a synonym or antonym for the word. Choose common prefixes and suffixes to add to the cards and then build words.

EXAMPLE: Look in your favorite dictionary for the listing of prefixes and suffixes. Common prefixes are: pre, un, dis, non, post and re. Common suffixes are: ing, ed, es, ful, ness and ly.

IMPORTANT WORDS: Another excellent source of 'words to know' is the Dolch word list. The Dolch list is prepared by grade and is a wonderful guide for parents and teachers. Examine the Dolch word list to determine which basic words your child should know. EXAMPLE: When children finish third grade, they should know all of the words through and including the 'third-grade list.' The cards can be purchased in a teacher supply store in your area.

REMEMBER: Games such as "Ring-A-Letter" reinforce phonics and word-attack skills that will help children crack the code of the English language. This game can be fun for the whole family as the children become better readers.

A-B-C-D-E-F-G

CRACK THE CODE - #14
Word Wizard

Word Wizard reinforces phonics, word-attack skills and vocabulary development from word lists such as the Dolch word list. Dolch word lists are available at teacher supply stores or the schools. Dolch lists are excellent teaching tools for parents and teachers. Each list provides words students should know at a particular grade level.

In "Word Wizard" the parent needs a word list appropriate for each player. It could be words that provide practice in consonants, vowels-a, e, i, o, u or blends such as bl, gl, sn, tr. Or, Word Wizard could be aimed at practice of spelling words or Dolch words. This game can be applied to a variety of skills. If you are not sure which is appropriate, ask the child's teacher.

POINTERS FOR PARENTS

MATERIALS NEEDED

- List of ten words for each player: After you decide whether to practice vowel sounds, blends or whole words, make a list of ten words. If you choose words, refer to words from a school list, or Dolch list for the child's grade level.
- Old magazines or newspapers
- Scissors and glue

SETUP

- Provide a word list for each player.
- Have plenty of magazines, newspapers and scissors.

THE GAME:

If you choose **Dolch words or spelling words** the player will be looking for that word in the newspaper or magazine. Once found, they will cut the word or picture out. They can place the words in an envelope or paste them on a poster.

If you choose **vowel sounds** such as long o in the word 'rope,' the child will be looking for words that rhyme with rope such as hope or cope. If you choose blends such as 'bl,' the child will look for words that contain that blend.

Do you see how this activity can be applied to just about any skill? The entire family can participate.

TIME LIMIT

- Allow about 15 minutes.
- At the end of 15 minutes each player shares the picture and the word discovered.

BONUS POINTS

- Award 5 bonus points for each word used correctly in a sentence.

POSTERS

- Paste pictures or words on poster board or construction paper and hang them on the bedroom walls.
- Or, put them in a brown envelope that clasps and decorate it. Save it; you can use it again for another activity.

REMEMBER: Games such as 'Word Wizard' reinforce phonics and word-attack skills that will help children crack the code of the English language. This game can be fun for the whole family as the children become better readers. You'll be gratified when you become involved in the children's learning.

CRACK THE CODE - #15
Sound Block

SOUND BLOCK

In "Sound Block" the parent needs a word list or skill list appropriate for each player. It could be words that provide practice in consonants (all the letters excluding the vowels), vowels (a, e, i, o, u) or blends such as bl, gl, sn, tr. Or, "Sound Block" could be aimed at practice of spelling words or Dolch words. This game can be applied to a variety of skills. If you are not sure which is appropriate, ask the child's teacher. If your child is of preschool age, begin with the letters of the alphabet and the sounds they make.

MATERIALS NEEDED

- Small building blocks
- Supplies to print or paste letters or words
- Square of felt or other soft material

SETUP

- Skill or word list for each player
- Floor area for players and blocks

THE GAME:

On each side of the building block print or paste one of six letters that the children will use. Sit in a circle on the floor. One child sits in the center and tosses the block on the soft material. When the block stops the child in the center names the letter and calls on another child to name a word that begins with the sound the letter represents. If working with whole words, players will pronounce the word. If correct, the child may have the next turn to toss the block. If incorrect, the child in the center calls on someone else to answer.

If you choose **vowel sounds** such as long o in the word 'rope,' the child will state words that rhyme with rope such as hope or cope. If you choose blends such as 'bl,' the child will pronounce words that contain that blend.

Do you see how this activity can be applied to just about any skill? The entire family can participate.

BONUS POINTS

- Award 5 bonus points for each word used correctly in a sentence.

IMAGINATION

- Create your own variations of this game to create collages, posters or stories with the words being used.
- Children will have suggestions in this category.

REMEMBER: Games such as 'Sound Block' reinforce phonics and word-attack skills that will help children crack the code of the English language. This game can be fun for the whole family as the children become better readers. You'll be gratified when involved in the children's learning.

♦ CULTURAL LITERACY ♦

Who was George Washington? Why do we celebrate the Fourth of July? Can you recite our Pledge of Allegiance? Who was Mark Twain? Who was Scarlet O'Hara?

If you can answer these questions, you are culturally literate. You have a common knowledge base, expected of literate Americans. To be a completely literate person, readers need to be culturally literate first. If readers do not have a knowledge base common to the writers,' comprehension of the printed page is difficult.

The readers' cultural literacy is what they bring to the printed material as they read. Cultural literacy is the information, facts and events we have been taught about our culture or heritage.

EXAMPLES OF CULTURAL LITERACY:

EXAMPLE 1: Thomas Jefferson said it best in his letter to Colonel Edward Carrington, January 16, 1787 in *The Life and Selected Writings of Thomas Jefferson:*

"Were it left to me to decide whether we should have a government without newspapers, or newspapers without a government I should not hesitate a moment to prefer the latter. But I should mean that every man should receive those papers and be capable of reading them."

The cultural literacy the reader needs to understand the excerpt is: Who is Thomas Jefferson? If the reader knows who Thomas Jefferson is, the importance of literacy vs. government becomes clear.

EXAMPLE 2: In the Lifestyles section of our local newspaper a few years ago, an advertisement for the television show "Designing Women" read:

"In a final episode of Designing Women, the four Atlanta interior decorators will imagine what life might be like if they were Scarlet O'Hara."

The cultural literacy needed to understand this is: Who is Scarlet O'Hara? What does this character have to do with four Atlanta interior decorators?

POINTERS FOR PARENTS

1. Determine your children's cultural literacy level. Ask a few basic questions such as 'What is the real meaning of the Fourth of July?' 'Who was George Washington?'
2. If you feel your children are lacking in cultural literacy, visit the public library for books on our national heroes and culture.
3. Celebrate national holidays such as the Fourth of July and Memorial Day with the family. Be sure to teach the meaning of such holidays. The schools may not be teaching it.
4. Ask the school staff what they are doing to teach cultural literacy. Be prepared to explain the definition of cultural literacy.

REMEMBER: To be completely literate, readers need cultural literacy. Readers need a similar knowledge base to take to the printed page. Writers assume a certain level of cultural literacy in their readers. As parents, we can help prepare our children.

♦ THE COMPREHENSION CONNECTION ♦

PARENTS, ONE THING we should always remember is that when we took the job of parenting we also accepted the responsibility to be our children's first teachers. As parents, we are always helping, directing and explaining what is right and what is wrong. We are constantly trying to help our children understand things. The values we instill, the direction we give, will last a lifetime. One of the most important 'understandings' we can instill is understanding to read. Your first reaction may be: "I'm not a teacher, how can I teach my children to understand what they read?"

It really is quite simple to include some activities in our homes. The activities will not cost anything—only some time. And of course, as parents, we know we need to provide time.

First, we need to know that reading is a process skill. It takes many years to master reading. In the beginning years of reading children are learning to read; in the later elementary years, children are reading to learn. What we hope is that our children will reach the second stage, reading to learn, while in the fourth grade. If they do, they are right on schedule.

Second, reading is a very complex series of skills. There are many layers and many facets. Depending upon the age and ability of our children we can ensure that certain activities occur.

Third, one of the most important reading skills we need is the skill of comprehension. To comprehend is to understand and give meaning to what we read. As we are reading, we have all experienced distractions and interruptions. It is even more difficult for the child who is just learning the steps to reading success.

In addition to being immersed in reading programs at school, there is much we can do at home to reinforce or instill the skills needed. Even though our children are all at different developmental stages of reading, there are some basic ideas we can incorporate into our home. As the parent, tailor the activities to best suit the child.

Let's review a few basics:

1. **Emphasize** the left-to-right movement. Reading is a left-to-right skill and children need to differentiate between right and left. Play as many games as you can think of to reinforce right and left. A few of my favorites are the floor game of Twister and Hokey Pokey circle dance.
2. **Read together** and read aloud often. Practice, practice, practice with the children and show them the parents like reading, too!

HINT: Major rule of thumb is: If they don't have the reading basics by the third grade, they will be playing catch-up the next nine years.

POINTERS FOR PARENTS

COMPREHENSION CONNECTIONS

1. Parental logic is needed here—parents need to have some idea of what types of books are appropriate for the child. Ask the librarian or school for advice for your child.
2. Spend time reading with the child. After you read a page or a paragraph, close the book and ask: "What is the boy's name? What is this story all about? Where is this taking place?"
3. Ask the basic 'w' and 'h' questions throughout the story or book: *Who* is in the story? *When* does it take place? W*here* does it take place? *What* is going on? *Why* do you think this is happening? *How* do you think the story will end?

4. The where and when questions are usually answered in the very beginning of the story, or book. Look for them as they read aloud or as you read aloud to them.

5. Groups of words: As the child enters third grade she/he should be in the process of mastering 'phrasal reading': grouping 3-4 words together for meaning, or comprehension. Prior to third grade, children read *one* word at a time. The 'one word at a time' reading should begin to disappear and 'phrasal reading' should begin. For example: Instead of reading *one word at a time* in this sentence *small groups of meaning* should be discovered *by the reader*. The word groups previously underlined or italicized should be taken in by the eyes at a single glance. This phrasal reading is the beginning of comprehending what we read. As an effective adult reader, we do this automatically. If your child is in fifth or sixth grade and is still reading one word at a time, she/he needs comprehension help. Practice the 'phrasal reading' with the children and continue to ask those *five w* questions with the *h* question. Contact the school for more specific guidelines for your child.

REMEMBER: Any help we can give our children to be successful readers is well worth our time. Reading is a life-long skill. Once reading is mastered, other subjects seem manageable.

♦ CREATE A READING-FRIENDLY HOME ♦

As parents, continue to reinforce the difference between right and left, categorizing and organizing. In addition, it is important to have a reading-friendly environment. If reading is seen as a part of the parents' day and an integral part of the home, it will become a natural for the children to incorporate reading into their lives. The more natural and friendly the process of reading is for children, the easier they will absorb the necessary skills and training. Children then develop a positive mind-set toward reading. Once this is accomplished, the children develop a love of reading with a natural desire to learn more about it. They will then be self-motivated. To create a reading-friendly environment may require only some rearranging of materials and time.

If we remember that reading is to the mind what physical exercise is to the body, then we will remember the importance of creating an environment conducive to reading. An inviting reading environment takes many shapes and forms. It is important to keep in mind the age of your child and the child's favorite colors and interests.

The creation of this reading-friendly atmosphere is not costly. It merely requires some rearranging and imagination. Involve the entire family in the discovery and creation of a reading place for everyone.

POINTERS FOR PARENTS

1. Set a good example: Scatter reading material on your favorite coffee table. Place it in plain view so all can see the value you place on reading.
2. Reserve a special time for reading your magazines or books. Be sure it is a time when the children see you reading.

3. Designate a place where you do your best reading. Comfort and good lighting are important. My husband and I both love to read. There are books and magazines in various locations in our house: on the coffee table and in the bookcase. I recently designed a corner just for me and my reading. I moved one of our existing chairs and footstool to a cozy corner. I placed one of our lamps in the corner, dusted and cleaned the area. Then I placed one of our cream-colored afghans over the arm of the chair, and rearranged the books on the small shelf to my right. I found an ivory Victorian-lace curtain I no longer use, which I stapled to the wall adjacent to the chair. It looks very inviting! I get excited when I gather my book and cup of coffee and head for the chair. My reading corner has created one problem: My husband finds it equally inviting and often scurries to the chair with his book first. I guess that, in itself, is proof I created an inviting, well-lit, comfortable place for reading. Our next project will be to create a reading area just for him.

4. Use supplies you already have. Children love the idea of large pillows on the floor or beanbags. Children have great ideas to make a place on the floor!

5. Find an old refrigerator box from an appliance store. Supervise the decoration of it with the children. The children could color it, paint it or glue some of their posters to it. A corner of their bedroom is a good area. Do not use the bed they sleep in—we want to invite reading, not sleeping.

6. Visit the local library. Assist your child in the selection of books of interest to them. The librarian can become your resource. She/he can keep you informed of new arrivals and help your children with their selections.

HAVE FUN WITH IT!

REMEMBER: The parent is the child's first teacher. Parents teach by example. What we do, children see and remember. If we show that we like to read and design places where our best reading can take place, our children will most likely develop a love of reading. If the children love to read, they will have a much greater chance of succeeding in their school years and beyond.

LITERACY AND CRACK THE CODE CONCLUSION

I hope the literacy articles and the Crack the Code series have provided you with useful information to enhance literacy awareness, knowledge and practice in your home.

Even though the schools have the primary responsibility to teach reading during the elementary years, parents can create a solid foundation of reading readiness during the preschool years. If the activities mentioned are implemented in the home, the child will be better equipped to achieve reading success.

REMEMBER: Once children are taught the secrets to crack the code of our language, they begin to attach meaning to the printed word. They begin to experience the joys of reading.

To Order Books

Please Send:

__________ *Copies of* The Encyclopedia of Parenting From A-Z, *So Help Me God!*

at $17.95 each Total ____________________

Shipping/Handling

$2.50 for first book ____________________

$1.50 each additional ____________________

TOTAL ENCLOSED ____________________

Name ____

Address ____

City __________________________St _____ Zip__________

Send cash, check or money order to:

Dr. Carol Kennedy
P.O. Box 51518
Fort Myers, FL 33994-1518

Dr. Kennedy is available for consulting and speaking engagements.
You may visit her web site at: www.drcarolkennedy.com
Or, e-mail her at: drckennedy@aol.com
Or call toll free 1-888-291-5605, pin# 7309